THE SECRETS OF PRICEWISE

ACKNOWLEDGEMENTS

Thanks to Nick Pulford, whose original plan for this book
was invaluable; to Mark Coton, Mel Collier and Tom Segal
for talking so frankly about their Pricewise experiences;
to James Pugh, who raided the *Racing Post* archives in search
of early columns; and to all the bookmakers, readers and colleagues
who gave up their time to be interviewed.

THE SECRETS OF PRICEWISE

THE WORLD'S NUMBER ONE RACING TIPSTER REVEALED

JAMES MILTON

RACING POST

Published in 2012 by
Racing Post Books
Axis House, Compton, Newbury, Berkshire, RG20 6NL

10 9 8 7 6 5 4 3 2 1

A catalogue record for this book is available from the British Library.

ISBN 978-1-908216-42-7

Cover designed by Jay Vincent
Designed by Fiona Pike

Printed and bound by CPI Group (UK) Ltd, Croydon, CR0 4YY

www.racingpost.com/shop

CONTENTS

INTRODUCTION

THE HALF-YEARLY reports from major companies tend to concentrate on market forces and global trends rather than the actions of individuals. The occasional rogue trader or white-collar criminal might receive an ignominious mention but, generally, these reports make for dry reading. In September 2005, however, the chief executive of William Hill broke with tradition by publicly blaming a newspaper tipster for the bookmakers' disappointing results.

"It could have been better," David Harding told his shareholders. "Pricewise tipped a winner for ten weeks running and the *Racing Post* turned it into a 'bash the bookies' campaign. I'm delighted to say his winning run came to an end on Saturday. It could have been better if it wasn't for him."

Harding's quotes were certainly newsworthy. The story brought a dash of colour to the financial pages of *The Daily Telegraph* and *The Guardian* while the *Daily Mirror* summed up the bookies' announcement with the headline "William Hell!" While the *Mirror* may have overplayed the story a little – William Hill's six-month profits had been dented but it was still in rude health – there was no doubt that Pricewise, the *Racing Post*'s flagship tipping column, wielded enormous power in the British betting industry.

Tom Segal, the tipster whose ten consecutive winning Saturdays cost the industry millions of pounds in the summer of 2005, was already admired and feared by bookmakers in equal measures. During an earlier run of winners for Segal, in 2003, Bet Direct spokesman Matthew Stubbs had admitted that "like most bookmakers, we live in fear of Pricewise. If we are in black type as the biggest price [about a horse that Segal has tipped] our legs tend to go a bit wobbly. We regard Pricewise as the most influential tipping service in the world. We've got nothing but admiration for it – through gritted teeth."

"It's the same for all bookmakers now," Skybet's Dale Tempest confirmed. "You put your prices in to the *Racing Post* on Friday and hope you are not standout on the Pricewise selection the next day. You have got to be prepared to lay them and it makes a real difference to the day. Pricewise can make the difference between a winning or a losing week."

The influence of Pricewise is testament to the consistency and brilliance of the three tipsters who have written the column since its inception in February 1987. Back then, its objective of highlighting value bets among the early prices offered by bookmakers was regarded with some suspicion. Now, thanks to the efforts of founder Mark Coton, his successor Mel Collier and the incumbent Tom Segal, Pricewise is an established brand, respected and loved by punters throughout Britain and Ireland.

All three men have been interviewed in depth for this book. The first three chapters document their memories of the Pricewise job and their approach to betting on racing. In Chapter Four, Segal offers his advice for profitable punting and Chapter Five follows Pricewise through one of the most hectic weeks of the racing year: the Cheltenham Festival. Bookmakers, professional punters, *Racing Post* colleagues and loyal readers also share their thoughts on the tipping column that Graham Sharpe of William Hill calls "the experts' expert."

Any celebration of Pricewise is also a celebration of the centuries-old battle between punters and bookmakers. Pricewise has been fighting that good fight for more than a quarter of a century and, sadly for the bookies, its appetite for winners shows no sign of waning.

THE EARLY YEARS

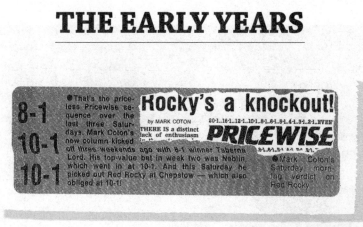

The Racing Post's *front page on February 23, 1987 hails a perfect start for its new tipping service, Pricewise.*

ON FEBRUARY 7, 2007, the *Racing Post* published a feature marking the 20th anniversary of the first Pricewise tipping column. Among the articles which celebrated "the column that was to make its own newspaper headlines and become the world's most successful tipping service" was an interview conducted by Peter Thomas with the creator of Pricewise, Mark Coton. The headline hailed Coton as "the man who changed the face of tipping." Two decades earlier, however, he was just another aspiring racing journalist who had messed up a job interview with Graham Rock, the *Post*'s founding editor.

"I was working in the marketing department of Ladbrokes at the time," Coton recalls. "I'd snuck away for an interview with Graham Rock and his deputy Francis Kelly and I didn't think it had gone very well. In fact, I knew it hadn't because Francis had gone through a list of about 20 questions – which horse won the Cesarewitch in 1962? Is there a round mile at Beverley? – and I didn't know the answer to half of them. Midway through the interview I realised that my chances of a job were disappearing into a black hole. I couldn't answer any of Francis's questions and Graham was just sitting there, not saying anything. So I decided to gamble and I told them that what interested me wasn't what had won ten years ago but what would win tomorrow.

"As it turned out, I didn't get the job. I was rejected. But we'd also done a written test and the story I heard is that Paul Johnson, the football

Mark Coton, the founder of Pricewise and "the man who changed the face of tipping"

tipster, saw my test and told either Francis or Graham that they ought to rethink their decision. They changed their minds at the last minute and one evening I received a telephone call from Graham, offering me a position on the bottom rung of the ladder as a junior writer.

"By this point I'd been made redundant by Ladbrokes. I'd been there for less than a year. One morning I arrived to find the desk being carried out of my office with all my papers still on top of it, which wasn't a very nice thing to see, even if I hadn't liked the job much! So when Graham rang me up – it must have been shortly before Christmas 1985 – I was in abeyance. I had no job and I accepted his offer in an unseemly hurry."

The mid-1980s was an exciting time to be a young racing journalist. Rock, backed by Sheikh Mohammed's millions, was assembling a team at the *Racing Post* that would take on – and ultimately usurp – its venerable rival *The Sporting Life*. *The Daily Telegraph*'s 2001 obituary of Rock, written by one of his protégés, JA McGrath, captured the spirit of the period: "Many racing journalists were indebted to [Rock] for giving them their start in journalism. His generosity knew no bounds and in the early days of the *Racing Post* he created a happy, frantic and exhilarating atmosphere."

It was an atmosphere that suited Coton. "I'm not a company man, really," he admits. "I'm a bit of an individualist. But the *Post* was the most fantastic place to work because all sorts of people were there – tabloid journalists, people from Timeform, old racing journalists and then a whole raft of people who seemed to have come from nowhere. The juniors were myself, Emily Weber, JA McGrath, who now does the television commentary and writes for the *Telegraph*, and a fellow called Lawrence Wadey, who later moved out to Hong Kong. After a few months Paul Hayward [later chief sports writer at *The Daily Telegraph*] joined the sports team. There was an incredible body of talented people and it was a real melting pot."

Coton includes himself among those "who seemed to come out of nowhere" but his interest in racing was no fluke. "It was in the family," he says. "My grandfather on my mother's side was a big racing fan and a part-time bookmaker and there were bookies on my father's side as well. But betting wasn't mentioned at all at home. It wasn't popular with my parents, perhaps because my grandfather lost a lot of money. He was badly injured in the First World War and I think he lost a few quid late in his life.

"Betting was definitely bubbling away under the surface, though. I'd always watch 'Grandstand' and wonder what '10-1 bar' and all those other phrases meant and it was a world that intrigued me, probably because it was forbidden. In the summer of 1976, when I was 14, I'd go into the arcades in St Ives and play the pinball machine, the fruit machines, and when I got bored of them I'd go up the steps to the bookies. In those days you couldn't see in through the windows but there were these straggly little bits of metal to let in the air when the shop became too smoky. I was looking into this mysterious world, through this kind of veil, and I knew at once that it was where I'd go on and do something in life."

That romanticism would remain with Coton throughout his career in betting, mingling with a sense of self-reliance and the desire to do things his own way. "I started to develop my interest in racing on my own," he says. "First of all I went to Warwick, which was where it was first triggered although I still wasn't allowed to mention it at home. I went to the London School of Economics and I was an idealist. I wanted to change the world but from a career point of view I didn't know whether I was going to be a barrister or a politician or a campaigner – somebody like Des Wilson, who set up the charity Shelter, for example. So while I was at the LSE there was this ongoing tension between what was expected of me – nobody in our family had been to university before and there was pressure on me to do law and become a barrister – and the racing side. And I didn't have any doubt that I could shine in racing. It wasn't an egotistical thing, I just knew that I wanted to be the first name on the team sheet, if you like, and racing seemed to be the obvious field. But there were always the two competing paths – racing and the law."

The first team sheet to bear Coton's name was that of *Trainers Record*, a statistical journal founded in 1973 by Peter Jones, who would later become chairman of the Tote. "It was the best schooling you could possibly have," Coton says. "Peter just let us get on with it. We'd have to compile our own handicaps, write comments, write essays, do all sorts. I started at *Trainers Record* in 1982 and worked there for two years. There were only three of us there at that time but Mel Collier [Coton's successor as Pricewise] also worked there later on. When I started, Peter was hardly around at all because he was working for an advertising agency, so we just had to get on with it."

Despite landing his first job in racing, Coton was still uncertain about which career path to pursue. "At the same time as I was working at *Trainers Record*, I met Paddy Ashdown. He was the Liberal candidate for Yeovil and I was living in the constituency. One afternoon I was watching the rugby on television and I saw a fellow in a flak jacket walking down the street with a folder in his hand. I told my friend that this guy must be the keenest double-glazing salesman we'd ever meet but it turned out to be Paddy Ashdown. I explained to him that I'd only just moved to the area but that I wanted to work for him.

"One possible career path was that I would stand for the county council and then go to Cornwall to try and win a seat but when Ashdown got elected he was absolutely appalled by the House of Commons. He came back and said it was like the worst kind of gentlemen's club. So I'd had it all planned out and then I just demolished it because I realised it wasn't going to work. I didn't want to spend eight years like Ashdown had – a man of his ability – beavering away, preparing the ground to get the base to win. It was all planned out but I just demolished it."

Banishing thoughts of Westminster, Coton went instead to Harrow, where he joined the marketing department of Ladbrokes in 1985. "I hated it," he admits, "because, as I said, I'm not a company man. I didn't like it there at all. I didn't fit in and they didn't like me but in hindsight, as the second part of my schooling, it was another great education. I got to see how bookmakers worked from the inside. You were supposed to stick to your own department but I was inquisitive so I often used to go into the trading department to try and pick up what was going on in there."

One illicit trip to the trading room during the 1985 Cheltenham Festival proved to be a significant milestone in the history of Pricewise. "In those days bookmakers only had a few early prices, even at Cheltenham," Coton recalls. "Ladbrokes had priced up West Tip as an 8-1 shot in the three-mile handicap. They were the top price about the horse, I think because Cyril Stein [the chairman of Ladbrokes] didn't fancy him. He used to say, 'Oh, this isn't going to win – we can just lay this one.' But there were all sorts of voices being raised in the trading department because West Tip was being backed throughout the day. It was a public gamble – it won at 4-1 or 7-2 – and I remember thinking it would have been good to give that in the paper. If I could have tipped that one, well, it would knock everything else down. That's where the seed was planted in terms of Pricewise, I think. Because, of course, it demonstrated to me that bookmakers were fallible. They were furious when West Tip won. The trading director threw a cup of coffee out of the window!"

By the time of the next Cheltenham Festival, Coton had started work at the *Racing Post*. The first edition of the paper was published on April 15, 1986 but it was soon apparent to Rock's staff that it would have to fight hard for survival. "I think there had been an assumption that *The Sporting Life* would fold because it was creaking beyond repair," says Coton. "In fact, though, the *Life* mounted a really rather fantastic rearguard action and very quickly it became clear that there was a mighty battle for circulation and that the *Post* was not going to have the field to itself. Having worked for a bookmaker, I knew that the market for betting and racing is very rigid. It's a very stubborn market. People don't change habits easily. Look at punters in betting shops – they're still backing the same kind of horse they were backing 25 years ago. So people weren't just going to switch from the *Life* to the *Post* even if we'd been really good, which we weren't at first."

Inevitably, the *Racing Post* required time to find its feet and establish its own identity. "It was in tabloid form," explains Coton "but there were various competing tendencies at the paper. There was a tabloid mentality, a broadsheet mentality, a Timeform mentality as well as a heap of people, like me, who were just ambitious. They had just turned up there and would run with anything."

Coton's own ambition to become a tipster was frustrated by his lowly rank at the paper. "Originally I was just a floater," he says. "I didn't have a fixed role because I was only a junior. The tipping group was in one corner and all the tipping jobs were taken – nothing doing there – so I went to work on the production desk under Francis Kelly, doing the cards and the form. Once the paper started in 1986, that was my job, and after about six months of that I was thinking 'I could be here for years'.

"It was all demarcated. All the tipsters and writers were in place and I didn't know how I was going to get noticed. I think Francis had told me to read everything that Harold Evans [the former *Sunday Times* editor] had ever written about journalism. One thing that Evans always said was that a journalist is somebody who makes a nuisance of themselves. There was a radical, individual streak running through people like Evans and Hugh McIlvanney, the great sports writer. They did their own thing.

"So I was always badgering the news desk, asking if there were any stories to write, and eventually they gave me one. They wanted 15 or 20 pars about a big Cheltenham handicap in December and the chief sub-editor Peter Hilton told me to ring the trainers for their quotes and then ring the bookmakers for their prices. When I'd done that I thought to myself 'well, what's the story here?' And I reckoned that the most interesting news angle was that one particular horse, Oregon Trail, was overpriced. I wrote the story – they hadn't asked for a tip, remember – saying that Oregon Trail was too big a price and I fully expected the piece to go on the spike. There literally used to be a spike in the corner of the office in those days and I expected Peter to come over and say 'what the hell is this all about? I wanted a news story and you're tipping this horse.'

"I hadn't been asked for a tipping piece but I wrote one anyway because to me that was the story. The most dynamic and interesting news angle was not that some trainer had said 'this is a nice horse, we've got it ready' – yawn, yawn, yawn. It wasn't an opportunity to give a bit of PR to the bookmakers and put their prices in the paper for free. The concrete reality, the dynamic, living news story was that this particular horse was a big price. It was a mistake by the bookmakers. It was a rick and when I was working at Ladbrokes that was what they used to hate most of all. The worst sin in the trading department was to make a rick. Anyway, they actually ran the story in the paper and the horse shortened in the betting and won. Another little seed was planted and I started to put together the idea for a tipping column."

Despite the triumph of that unconventional news story – or the fact that it was, at least, spared the spike – the *Racing Post*'s approach to tipping remained stoutly traditional. "It's important to remember the background at that time," says Coton. "There was no internet, no online gambling, no exchanges. There was no computerised form. There wasn't even any televised racing in the betting shops – I think SIS only kicked in two or three years later. Betting tax was at nine per cent and, in terms of tipping, the supreme orthodoxy was a combination of Timeform and handicapping. The people who'd come to the *Post* from Timeform preached pounds-per-length handicapping, which then fused in to ratings, so that was the supreme authority, almost like the Pope. It was the prevailing orthodoxy.

"There seemed to be this idea that there was a 'correct' answer to a race. You'd be looking at the ratings, studying various calculations and if you were any good you'd come out with the right horse – the professional selection, filtered through the handicapping and underpinned by sound reasoning. But because Lawrence Wadey and I had worked at *Trainers Record* we'd never done that sort of pounds-per-length stuff. I think Peter Jones told us not to look at Timeform until the very last minute otherwise we'd just come up with the same answers as they had. I'm not sure if we even had Timeform in the office at *Trainers Record*.

"When Lawrence and I were looking at a race, our first question would be 'is there a bet here?' That was totally alien to the other tipsters at that time. Tipping wasn't supposed to be about what you fancied or what was the best value – it was about doing the research and coming up with the 'correct' horse. The other tipsters worked really hard and got stuck into the form whereas I was just looking for the sort of horse that I'd like to back."

Coton's disdain for orthodoxy was still apparent in 2008 when he was asked by the *Racing Post* to recall his best ever bet. He nominated a

Graham Rock, the Racing Post's *founding editor, authorised the launch of Pricewise*

loser – Sweet Mover, who was narrowly beaten in the Extel Handicap at Goodwood in August 1986. It was his best bet "in technical terms" because he had spotted a horse that no other tipster had considered, backed it at 20-1 in the morning and also tipped it to his editor Graham Rock.

The fact that Sweet Mover was nabbed late on by Luca Cumani's Chinoiserie was "a sickening blow" at the time but Coton refused to be despondent about the near-miss. "What I learned," he wrote, "was that it matters like hell whether a certain horse wins a certain race but in the same moment it doesn't matter in the slightest. It's a little Zen-like, maybe. It was dreadful when the camera panned out to show Chinoiserie catching Sweet Mover, but it was also a marvellous feeling when I thought the horse was going to win and I had found a long-priced winner no-one else had spotted. That's what I focused on, and that's what I found to be important. The Sweet Mover episode also helped to open the door for Pricewise, which came along a few months later, with the perception of finding and highlighting a value bet that others might not have spotted. All in all, it was a pivotal bet in so many ways – even though it didn't win." And so the gallant runner-up Sweet Mover joined West Tip and Oregon Trail as a key equine figure in the prehistory of Pricewise.

Coton's first regular writing opportunity at the *Racing Post* was not Pricewise but a column called Better Betting. "My unique selling point was that I had worked for a bookmaker so I wangled a weekly column about the bookmaking industry," he says. "It appeared with a byline photo in which I looked about 15 – I hated it, I still hate all those ridiculous byline photos. Pricewise never had them when I was doing it. Anyway, the Better Betting column used to be very critical of the bookmakers, which is unthinkable now, of course."

Writing provocative columns gave Coton a start but, if he really wanted to inflict damage on the bookmakers, he needed a regular tipping piece. He was fortunate to be working alongside Francis Kelly, who had already spotted the potential of value betting on football coupons. "It was clear to me that Mark was a shrewd, bright guy," says Kelly. "He came to me with an idea for a tipping service based on early-morning prices and I was immediately interested because I'd tried a similar thing on football. I can't say if that influenced Mark directly but it probably meant that I felt more supportive towards his idea.

"Football betting as we know it began in 1975. For a decade before then there had been a 40 per cent tax on football betting but the bookies won a court case to have football taxed at the same rate as racing. The key to my success was that every single bookie was producing his own coupon so there would be some incredible discrepancies. Outrageous discrepancies – you'd have a match like QPR-Tottenham and Hills would go 13-8 QPR, 13-8 Tottenham while Ladbrokes would be 4-5 and 7-2.

"Bookmakers were complacent because in those days you still had to bet in five-timers but as the odds would accumulate in the punters' favour there would be some great-value prices. I don't know why I didn't become a multi-millionaire, really! They were the golden days of football punting, between around 1978 and 1983, and I wrote a football tipping column for *The Sporting Chronicle*. I think one year my tips in the *Chronicle* showed 100 per cent profit on turnover but it wasn't about my opinion – it was all based on great-value odds."

That detachment – the prioritising of objective value over opinion – struck a chord with Coton. "I ran the idea past Francis," he says. "I told him 'this is what we're going to do. We'll get the prices off the bookmakers, just the main four or five – Coral, Ladbrokes, Hills, Mecca, the Tote, maybe – and if there's one that's going to shorten, like Oregon Trail, we'll tip it.' Francis reckoned it was a good idea but he wasn't sure about it appearing in Saturday's paper because Friday was the busiest day on the production desk. So my job was to persuade him, and then persuade Graham Rock, that I could be spared an hour to do the column.

"We had a meeting – Graham, Francis and myself – and I pitched the idea to them. Graham understood. He was a punter, of course, so he had a glint in his eye but he did everything to knock it back at first. Eventually, in a weary kind of way, he said to Francis 'well, can we spare him for an hour to have a crack at this?' And Francis, to his great credit, said yes and he also came up with the name for it: Pricewise. But I only had an hour to do it – an hour to phone the bookmakers, scheme a space for it on the page I was laying out, and then write the column. I think Graham and Francis agreed to it just to keep me quiet! They thought I'd have a couple of losers and then it would all go away."

A small plug for the new column appeared on the *Racing Post*'s front page on February 7, 1987. "Punters looking for value mustn't miss Mark Coton's PRICEWISE, our new betting feature on page 23," it instructed readers. "Like the professionals, Pricewise examines the best prices in the bookmakers' morning lists, and gives you the best chance of making a profit out of your betting."

"The first column was on page 23 and the first selection, Taberna Lord, won," Coton recalls. "In fact anyone could have found that one because it was pretty obvious but it was a big price and it won. Then another one,

Red Rocky, won two weeks later but I'd tipped it at 13-2 and it won at 10-1 so that was a failure. You simply did not do that because you're showing that you can't read the market."

Not many tipsters are annoyed with themselves after giving a 10-1 winner but, from the very start, Coton had a strict set of self-imposed rules for a Pricewise tip. The fact that a horse which was 8-1 in the morning had gone off at 4-1 was just as important as whether it then won or lost. "It was about the market dynamics," he says. "Not form dynamics, that's left to the proper form experts. This was a column about market dynamics."

At a time when the vast majority of punters just wanted to know which horse was going to win, launching a column about market dynamics was brave and innovative. Like most innovations, it was initially regarded with suspicion. "I felt that Pricewise was a creature in quarantine for a long time," Coton admits. "It took about nine months to establish itself properly, to convince people that it was the real thing. A lot of the time I'd have a winner and people would say 'it's a fluke, it's a guess' or else nobody would be bothered. Conversely, though, there was quite intense hostility from outside the paper. I had people who claimed to be professional punters phoning up, blaming me for letting the secret out – 'What are you playing at? Why have you let the bookies have the secret?' Others would accuse me of working for Ladbrokes because I'd write that if a horse was 14-1 with Coral and only 8-1 with Ladbrokes, that was an objective indicator of the fact that it was going to shorten. But they'd ring up and say 'how much are they paying you?' which wasn't very nice."

Paul Kealy, now the *Racing Post*'s betting editor and a high-profile tipster himself, joined the paper as an office junior in 1987, the year that Pricewise was created. He also recalls the animosity that the new column provoked. "Mark's idea of pooling all the prices and pointing out the value made a fair bit of sense to me, as a punter," says Kealy. "It wasn't universally popular, though. The office was in Raynes Park and I remember some locals moaning that Mark was giving the game away, spoiling it for those punters who were already shopping around for the value. It took time for the bookmakers to get on board too because they were wary of having their ricks exposed in the paper. And you have to remember that Mark wasn't a big name back then. He was still making his way in the game so he had to ram the idea down people's throats.

"Mark did such a good job with Pricewise and he also brought the idea into the sports betting arena. When he tipped Wimbledon to win the FA Cup in 1988 at 40-1, it had nothing to do with his opinion. It was purely on price. I thought he was bonkers so I laid 40-1 to loads of people in the office – I practically had to take out a loan to pay them all! But Mark had spotted that it was the wrong price and he knew that if you backed enough wrong prices you'd make money over time."

Pricewise's growth was a slow-burning affair, as Francis Kelly confirms: "It was very much Mark's personal baby to begin with. It would just be tucked away in the corner of a form page where a hole had appeared. It had a great start, of course, with Taberna Lord, but it grew quite slowly. There were a few more winners, which helped the column establish itself, and it eventually moved forward in the paper."

Alan Byrne, later editor and chief executive of the *Racing Post*, believes that Pricewise had a decent chance of survival from the start. "I first became aware of it as a reader," Byrne says. "I observed the success of the column under Mark's early tenure and saw the degree to which it started to move the market. In those days the morning markets were far less sophisticated than they are now and bookmakers only priced up a few handicaps.

"Clearly, there were no exchanges and there were three or four different tissues that the bookies subscribed to. Punters used to turn on Teletext to see what prices were on offer for horses in handicaps and how the market was moving. So it was soon obvious to me that Pricewise was going to be very influential, because I could see the prices collapsing when Mark had tipped something. The prices he tipped at and the success he had early on meant that bookmakers were having to take evasive action – and, happily, there were readers making money from the column.

"Pricewise obviously enjoyed the big advantage of having first run at the early prices and that, combined with Mark's innate ability, sensible approach and good judgement as a tipster, meant that it always had a fair chance of success. However, it has probably exceeded everybody's expectations in terms of the degree of that success and its longevity."

For Coton, though, there was always a sense of struggle during the early years. "It didn't fall ready-made from the sky," he says. "It's like any new idea – look at Harry Potter, for example. A lot of people said 'who's going

THE EARLY YEARS 21

to be interested in a story about a kid with glasses who's a wizard at a public school?' These things take time. It took nine months until I felt that Pricewise was anything other than an indulgence which I was allowed because I was a bit of a nuisance. Beau Ranger winning the Mackeson Gold Cup in November 1987 was an important moment. That was a proper horse in a proper race and I'd told everybody to have a proper bet."

Later, under Mel Collier and Tom Segal, Pricewise would become renowned for big-priced winners but Coton's approach was less flashy. "Sometimes, of course, I'd indulge myself and put up an outsider when I was trying to be clever but it was basically about pointing people towards a horse that they were going to fancy anyway," he explains. "I think Mel and Tom took it in a different direction but I wasn't trying to persuade people to back something that they hadn't thought about. I was just saying 'take the 6-1, take the 5-1, because it's going to start at 7-2.' After the first couple of months I'd always give an approximate starting price in the column, tell the readers what I thought the SP would be. Because that, to me, gave it an objective quality. If I'd said the SP would be around 4-1 and it was 8-1, then I'd be the one who had made a rick, not the bookmakers. The whole idea would be turned on its head."

Coton's task was not an easy one. He had to outsmart the bookmakers and anticipate market moves each Friday while also managing his production duties. There was no point putting in too much homework for such an acutely price-sensitive column because the bookmakers' odds could instantly render it useless. Instinct was more valuable than studiousness. "Before calling the bookmakers I'd look at a race and put a price on each horse's head, but without thinking about it too much," Coton says. "I'd pick out three or four horses that were interesting to me but I'd actually try not to have too strong an impression of what I fancied. I'd just mark down the prices I was hoping for and seven or eight times out of ten I'd have to scrap it all when the bookies' prices started coming over. There would be one that I'd think was a great 5-1 shot but when the prices arrived it was no bigger than 7-2 so I'd have to leave it alone.

"What I was really trying to work out was which horses were going to shorten. One guide to that was what Ladbrokes had done and another was the selections box that would appear on the news desk. One thing I knew from working at Ladbrokes was that *The Sun*'s tips had quite a weighty bearing on the market, and *The Sun*'s nap especially. So if there was a 14-1 shot that Templegate had napped and Ladbrokes were only 9-1 about it, you could be pretty sure that there'd be plenty of money for it. In the end I'd only have ten minutes to work out the angle – you've got to give them a form angle, throw something to the orthodoxy – and write the piece."

Those crucial ten-minute spells produced enough winners to boost the column's profile and attract the interest of one of racing's most familiar faces. John McCririck spotted Pricewise's potential at an early stage. "I was attracted to it in the first place because it was terribly different," he says. "It was a different way of analysing races. I certainly thought it was punter-friendly and it was as revolutionary in its time as the idea of laying horses on Betfair was."

Coton identifies McCririck's support as a major factor in Pricewise's eventual acceptance. "They'd never mention it on Channel 4 like they do now – it wasn't part of the establishment then – but McCririck was keen on the idea," he says. "He phoned me up one day and asked why we weren't printing all the bookmakers' prices. I told him I didn't have the time or the space – I had to fit it on the form pages and I couldn't collate all the prices myself. But I think his impetus helped Pricewise slowly evolve into the shape it has now, with the grid of prices. And it gradually moved from the data pages to the front of the newspaper, albeit on page 14 or wherever."

Just as Pricewise was gaining a foothold in the minds of punters and pundits, however, Coton's own hunger for the game was waning. When asked about his decision to quit the column in December 1989, Coton refers to one of his heroes, whose own gambling tastes probably lean towards Atlantic City rather than Ascot. "Bruce Springsteen tells a great story," he says. "He's in a car, of course, one day and he's on the open road. He's got the girl, the recording contract, the hit record – he's got it all – but suddenly he feels this icy sensation on the back of his neck and he thinks 'now what?'

"You think when you're young that if you have a success it'll make you happy and fulfilled but it doesn't. Pricewise wasn't a career for me. I never got a penny out of it, never got a pay rise or anything but that didn't interest me. I'd wanted to write a column that would be the first thing people turned to in the morning. That was what I'd wanted to do in a betting context. After I'd achieved that, I faced the same question as Springsteen: now what? I wasn't interested in my profile as a tipster. I think the concept of Pricewise was good and I'm proud of that. I'm proud that I made it work. But then I wanted something else. I'd also had a good year on the betting side and I wanted to do other things. I wanted to work in other fields. So at the end of 1989 I thought 'what's the most exciting and interesting thing that I could do with my life?' And the most exciting thing was to give it up. To throw it all away. I wanted to be free again."

Something of a legend has grown around Mark Coton in gambling circles. Discussions on internet forums depict him as the Syd Barrett of tipping; a JD Salinger figure who turned his back on racing at the very height of his powers. In fact, he remains a passionate and thoughtful fan of the sport, albeit one who is based in St Ives, on the north coast of Cornwall, rather than in a racing hub such as Newmarket or Lambourn. Coton's eclectic post-Pricewise career included freelancing for the *Racing Post*, editing Raceform on Saturday and writing two acclaimed books, *Value Betting* and *100 Hints For Better Betting*. In 1993 he appeared at a Home Affairs Select Committee on gambling, lobbying for punters' rights in his role as chairman of NAPP, the National Association for the Protection of Punters.

In a 2007 interview with the *Racing Post*, Coton gave his views on how Pricewise and value betting had evolved. "The orthodoxy of handicapping has given way to a value orthodoxy," he claimed. "People say 'we don't want to be on this because it's 11-8.' There's nothing wrong with an 11-8 winner, and there's a sense in which Pricewise has made people think there is. It's become associated with big-priced, glory-boy winners. Somehow we've ended up turning our noses up at the favourites, and I don't like that. If there's anybody out there who fancies giving 6-4 shots regularly, that would be an interesting person to hear from. If somebody walked in and said 'Pricewise is all very well, but it was avant garde and it's become a bit mainstream – I'm giving you a 6-4 winner', I can just imagine the seismic ructions that would go on in the office. I don't know what the next big thing is, but it isn't value, because everybody's doing that now. I just worry that the person with the next big idea is wasting his time laying odds-on shots on Betfair."

Coton believes that the precise definition of the term 'value' has become murky over the years. "Value is not something that you subjectively throw in at the end of a piece to justify your educated guesswork," he says. "You can't just say 'I'm giving this because I think it's value.' It loses its objective quality then. I was as guilty of this as anybody because I didn't think through the whole idea of value carefully enough. I wrote a book called *Value Betting*, which I realised later was a misleading title because what I actually did was value tipping. Betting and tipping are different worlds and as a value punter I made the same mistakes as everybody else."

He admires the concept of betting exchanges but confesses that they leave him a little cold: "On Betfair you can take 6-1 in the morning and then lay it – or back it back, as we used to say – at 7-2 but that's never interested me, personally. I'm not interested in markets in that sense. Market dynamics, yes, but not trading within markets. Betfair is an extraordinary idea – a stunning idea, partly arising from Pricewise, I think, with the way the odds are presented. It has computerised the market, which is the essence of the game. You know, you're on the track, there's five minutes to go before the off, the bookies are chalking up their prices and you've got to get in there and have your bet at 8-1 before the price disappears. It's the quicksilver, mercurial essence of the game – the thrill and the agony of the gambler."

Coton certainly doesn't envy the celebrity status that Pricewise has bestowed on Tom Segal. "If I was in Tom's position I'd be profoundly embarrassed by it. Tom cuts a decent enough dash on the telly but I think there's now a sense of tension within the paper about whether it's Pricewise saying this or Tom Segal saying it. But that's a product of the age. We live in the age of opinion. I always think that tipping should be oracular – it shouldn't be a personal opinion, it should appear to come from some source.

"The original suspicion that was held against me was that I was a nobody. Nobody had ever heard of me so why should I be allowed to express my opinion in the racing newspaper? So I told Graham Rock that it didn't matter what I thought. Pricewise wasn't a vehicle for my opinion – it was a tipping concept. I explicitly said there should be no photo byline on Pricewise. It's got nothing to do with whether you look like a reliable bloke or a bit of a rogue or whether the readers want to go for a pint with you.

"My colleague Howard Wright advised me to use the word 'I' sparingly in my copy and I tried to follow that advice. Not because I didn't have a high opinion of myself – I probably did! – but because it wasn't about me. If I'd had to deal with the publicity that Tom does, I'd have run a mile. What interests me is the concept, the idea, not necessarily the individual voice or the biographical details. It was the idea of Pricewise that 'changed the face of tipping' and I just happened to be the vehicle for the idea. The main contribution I made was to force the idea through against opposition."

Coton has lived in Cornwall for almost a decade and for several years after his move to St Ives he didn't set foot on a racecourse. "I like change," he says. "I like to walk away and do something different so I didn't go racing at all for seven or eight years. Then I started to go again, just quietly, to the Midlands tracks where I started out. For me racing is usually to do with summer memories and the summer sunshine. It's like going to your first football match as a child when you first see the green turf and there's that hum of expectation in the crowd. There's that same hum at a racecourse and I love the way the sun glints on the white rails.

"I went to Worcester recently. I had a few quid in my back pocket and I just thought 'let's see if I can turn it into a few more quid and if not, well, it's a lovely day by the river, isn't it?' We were standing by the rails and, two yards away from us, AP McCoy was getting the leg up on the favourite. I said to my friend 'in what other sport do you get this close to a supreme champion?' You don't. It's fantastic, the living and breathing experience of betting and racing. That's what interests me now – not trying to be a big shot but starting again with a clean sheet. It's a great feeling."

Coton is undoubtedly inspired by the fresh start, the clean sheet, the different angle but he will remain, for many punters, inextricably linked to Pricewise. He had always maintained that the tipping concept was more important than any individual writer; his departure from the *Racing Post* in December 1989 would reveal whether the column could survive and prosper without its founder.

ESTABLISHING THE BRAND

Tipping doesn't get any better than this

The wonder of Pricewise

33-1

AS Heidi (right) and Inn At The Top jumped the last together in the Great Yorkshire Chase at Doncaster on Saturday, Pricewise followers already knew they were in the money.

Melvyn Collier's astonishing run of big-priced winners was guaranteed to continue as his morning advice for the race had been to back both the winner, Heidi, at 33-1 (2pts win) and runner-up Inn At The Top at 11-1 (2pts win) to register a marvellous 64-point profit on the race.

And, as regular followers will know, this was no flash in the pan. In November, in almost a dress-

rehearsal for events on Saturday, Pricewise advised two horses for the Hennessy Cognac Gold Cup at Newbury, with his 10-1 shot King's Road (2pts win), beating his 40-1 offering Gingembre (2pts win, 1pt place).

This truly is the column the bookies fear, so don't miss a special Pricewise service this week when, starting tomorrow, the four major races at the Cheltenham Festival—Champion Hurdle, Queen Mother Champion Chase, Gold Cup and Stayers' Hurdle—go under the microscope.

■*Great Yorkshire Chase report, page 53*

Inn At The Top (left) and Heidi – the two horses tipped by Mel Collier – jump the last together in the 2001 Great Yorkshire Chase at Doncaster.

AFTER MARK COTON'S DEPARTURE from the *Racing Post*, the question was not who should take over as Pricewise but whether the column should continue at all. Mel Collier, who would establish himself as Coton's successor after a somewhat messy interregnum, remembers that Pricewise was still viewed with some suspicion at the start of the 1990s.

"I had the impression that the powers-that-be didn't want this upstart Pricewise getting too much attention," Collier says. "We used to refer to them as 'the grown-ups' and there was definitely a sense that the grown-ups preferred solid, traditional tipsters such as Diomed or Spotlight to this weird Pricewise thing. They thought they'd let Mark do what he wanted – he was a kind of mad professor with a bee in his bonnet – but the main thrust of the paper, tipping-wise, was still a Timeform-style approach. Adrian Cook did Diomed so it would be intelligent analysis but quite formal and the Spotlight writers would back that up."

Alan Byrne, who was the *Racing Post*'s news editor from 1990 to 1992 before becoming editor in January 1993, remembers Pricewise's changing of the guard. "Mark finished at the end of 1989 and Mel took over while I was news editor," Byrne says. "Different people were doing Pricewise for a while and different people had a view that they should do it in the long term. Fortunately, Mel took it on and was a great success at it."

By the time Collier handed over the reins to Tom Segal a decade later, Pricewise would be established as the *Racing Post*'s main tipping column and value betting would be, in Coton's words, "an orthodoxy". However, it took time for bookmakers, rival publications – and, indeed, the *Racing Post* hierarchy – to appreciate the gem that was still hidden away in the bowels of the paper.

Collier himself was well aware of the value of Pricewise. "Mark had made a real success of the column and I always used to read it religiously," he says. "But after he left it just used to get shared out among the Spotlight writers. Maybe the bosses weren't sure if anybody was good enough to take over or maybe they wanted to reduce its profile so it wasn't 'Mark Coton's Pricewise', it was just Pricewise – I'm not sure.

"The column would suit some tipsters' personalities better than others. I always used to like doing it and I'd fight to do it during that year or so when we were churning it out between us. I had a few successes – Multum In Parvo in the Mackeson Gold Cup was a big winner for me – and I started doing it more regularly. Then somebody asked if I wanted to do it on a full-time basis, I said yes, and that was it."

Even as a child, Collier's love of racing was driven by his fascination with betting. "My family had no connection with racing, really," he says. "I became interested through the betting angle. A relative of my father's – he was called Mr Gamble, as is the way of these things! – loved his betting. He was a big, clichéd old guy with a flat cap, a huge Willie Carson fan, and

Mel Collier, long-serving Pricewise tipster and, according to one Racing Post *reader, 'pure magic'.*

he'd have four-timers and five-timers every day. But he also used to get the Raceform ratings on a Saturday. I'd drop round after school and chat to him about racing so that got me started, along with the odd shilling on the Grand National each year. I went to university in Norwich, which isn't too far from Newmarket and Yarmouth, and gradually became more and more interested in racing."

Collier studied English and American literature at the University of East Anglia but he had no firm plans after graduation: "I dropped off the educational conveyor belt and didn't know what to do. I drifted into accountancy for four months because that was what everybody else seemed to be doing but the more I thought about it, the more I wanted to do a job I'd enjoy so I started looking around for anything in racing.

"Peter Jones, who went on to become head of the Tote, got me into the industry. He was looking for people to do Raceform-type stuff and he'd put an advert in *The Sporting Life* – 'fresh young meat required for slave wages', that sort of thing! – and I thought it looked good. So I met Peter for a bizarre interview on the train up to Beverley. I think he told me to meet him in carriage two – it was all espionage-style, you know, 'I'll be wearing a green corduroy suit' – and he interviewed me on the train and then we watched the racing at Beverley together."

That unconventional interview led Collier to a tiny village in Dorset where *Trainers Record* was based. His duties ranged from writing brief, stat-heavy essays on trainers for a yearly book to producing formguides

Peter Jones, who gave both Mark Coton and Mel Collier their starts at Trainers Record

and racecards. "We got a good general grounding in the industry," he says. "We did form guides for *The Times*, racecards for Weatherbys and we were Betting Spy in *The Sun* for a while. Dominic Gardiner-Hill, who's now a handicapper, was there and Crispin de Moubray took me under his wing and showed me the rudiments of handicapping so it was a great introduction to a lot of different areas of work.

"Then Peter got the contract to supply the *Racing Post* with form and general statistics. I don't really know the politics of it but I think he agreed to sell them the whole database – people included! – and we all moved up to Raynes Park. We were a little independent team within the *Racing Post* for a while, carrying on with contracts for *The Times* and other things, but gradually the work for the *Post* took over. There was always work to do – there would be greyhound form and Irish form and people would be asking for some data on the French racing or whatever – but I soon moved over to the tipping side.

"Writing Spotlight was quite frightening at first because it involved doing the betting forecast, which was the hardest job in the world. If you got it right – which you did, say, 85 per cent of the time – nobody noticed. It was just the glaring errors that they picked up on. There might be some hot new trainer who had landed a couple of gambles that you hadn't heard about. So he'd have a runner with no decent form and you'd put it in the betting forecast as a rag and suddenly it would be 7-2 on the day. But I loved the immediacy of it. Go in, do a shift, watch the races the next day – it's either a triumph or a disaster – and that's it."

With the benefit of hindsight, Collier was a perfect fit for the Pricewise role. Open to new ideas and "weird theories", he was also greedy for information that would help him solve the "puzzle" of each race. "Mel was the most obvious person to take over from Mark and he was extremely successful at it," says Paul Kealy, *Racing Post*'s betting editor. "He used to bounce ideas off people – he was a great receptor – and one of his strengths was that he never had any preconceptions about a race. Everything was new to him when he was looking at a race. He'd be taking a new approach to it all. I used to get the train to work with him and he'd ask me what I fancied for a certain race and when I told him he'd say he'd never heard of it."

"I thought information was the key," says Collier. "Not in the sense of 'this thing's been flying on the gallops' but historical information, information about the trainer, the horse – does it go well fresh, does it prefer racing left- or right-handed? Lots of this stuff simply wasn't available then so it wasn't factored into the prices. So I'd canvas everyone's opinions – I'd often speak to Craig Thake about the trends, for example – because that was how I liked to work. At the end of all that I could still say 'no, forget it, I'll do this weird theory' or I could say 'three people are all telling me that this horse will stay so I'll tip it.' I'd still make my own mind up but I always liked to hear other people's opinions. That's why the Betfair markets are so efficient these days, because there are so many people coming from so many different angles and in the end they produce a near-perfect market."

Pricewise also reflected Collier's personal betting habits. "Instinctively, I'm looking for bad favourites," he explains. "That's always been my gut feeling, which happened to coincide very well with the idea of Pricewise. Of course, I fully appreciate that there can be 6-4 shots which are great value but I was always better at picking out a 12-1 shot that should be 7-1 rather than a 5-2 shot that should be 9-4. I was intellectually and emotionally drawn to the pursuit of big-priced winners and I think the column lent itself to that sort of approach."

Collier characterises his approach as "race-centred" and agrees with Kealy's observation about his lack of preconceptions. "I'd look at the race and would have to learn about the horses. Most people follow a horse throughout its career but I'll tip something and then three months later I'll have forgotten it. I don't want any baggage going into a race. If you've backed a horse that's finished second and you think it's unlucky, you might back it again and again. Whereas if you can see it for the first time, almost, in a particular race then it's easier to make an objective judgement about its chances.

"I'd say to myself 'here's the puzzle, it's called the 3.30 at Newmarket. What shape is it? What are you going to do with it? What's going to affect the outcome?' You've obviously got your basics – things like form, going, draw and speed figures. Actually, when I first started at the *Post*, speed figures were seen as a dangerous offshoot, usually practised by weird Yorkshiremen for some reason, who used to complain about the stalls being moved seven yards forwards or backwards. It was a dark art! But all that sort of stuff interested me.

"I was influenced by the ideas coming out of America, for example. I think Mark Coton actually put me on to the early Beyer-type books – Beyer on speed, Beyer on handicapping. There wasn't really any equivalent in England. We were still relying on historical biographies or bits of received wisdom – 'you need a front-runner at Brighton' or whatever. I liked the statistical side and American ideas such as bounce concept. If you graph a horse's performance and it goes up dramatically, the European reaction is that he's on the upgrade and he's going to keep improving. Whereas the Americans would say that he's done a peak effort there and he'll probably regress back to the mean next time out.

"I felt that working at the *Post* gave me an edge. I could ask the guys in the computer department to print out a copy of a horse's lifetime form for me. That's commonplace now but in those days it was still difficult to get hold of something like that. Say I was tipping on an Ascot handicap, I could look at a horse's lifetime form and see it had had five Ascot runs. I'd think 'hang on a sec, it was third in that one, it was fourth from the wrong side there and it was tenth there but the ground was against it' and that would help me to build up an overview. It also helped that I wasn't a Timeform disciple – I was happy to come from left-field, to absorb information and think differently about a race. And with Pricewise, of course, there was the value agenda, which was absolutely key. That meant if I felt a horse was a 4-1 shot I wouldn't tip it at 3-1 even if I really fancied it, which was one of the hardest parts of the job."

With value at the very heart of his approach, Collier was constantly on the lookout for factors that were underestimated by the betting public and the bookmakers. These factors would, in turn, reveal which horses were underbet. "I don't think there was anything revolutionary in the way I looked at it," he says. "It was just, perhaps, that I was stressing some things that the general view might not have taken into account."

Naturally, those factors are subject to change, particularly as information becomes more and more accessible. In his Pricewise days, Collier believed that jumps horses racing on the flat – and vice versa – were rarely given enough respect by the layers. "I certainly felt that horses switching codes tended to be underbet," he says. "Look at the Swinton Hurdle, which used to be a benefit for well-handicapped flat horses. Now everybody is aware of that so they price it up accordingly. Likewise with the Chester Cup or the Ascot Stakes – people know that the jumps horses are super-fit and the jumps trainers are as good, if not better, than flat trainers at getting them ready for those sort of races. The bias that used to exist doesn't exist anymore, which is why there's very little value in the jumps-to-flat or the flat-to-jump switches nowadays. I remember Nick Mordin wrote a piece about women jockeys on horses that were 4-1 or shorter. He found that if you backed them blind you'd make a profit because there was an inherent sexism among punters! And these were always the sort of angles that interested me."

Under Collier, Pricewise developed from an interesting sideline into the first port of call for punters looking for a big-race tip on a Saturday. "It definitely became the biggest tipping piece in the paper," he says. "I think one advantage it had in PR terms was that it was easier to publicise the winners in the next day's paper. You'd have a puff with the headline 'get on so-and-so at 12-1' and you could say 'Bang! We told you to back this!' Whereas a Spotlight writer might have had an excellent day, with a 7-1 winner and a 12-1 winner, but because they'd also had four losers it wouldn't get the same treatment.

"I think Pricewise was also directed at the punter far more. There wasn't the sort of cerebral debate about, say, how a horse's breeding would affect its chances in the Derby. But the basic reason it grew was because it had a few winners and people started following it. It felt like a big event, because it wasn't in the paper every day and because it was linked to the televised racing so people started to look out for Pricewise whenever there was racing on the telly. I feel there's a natural rhythm to the season and to the big races – you go from Chester to York to Ascot and so on – and Pricewise became a part of that rhythm.

"It started to get publicity from 'The Morning Line' on Channel 4. They'd point out that the Pricewise horse had been backed – it was cut, the cut was reported, and then more people would back it so it began to feed itself. Punters who'd got the early prices felt they were on the inside. It was fantastic for them if they'd backed one at 10-1 or 12-1 and then it went off at 6-1 and won."

"Over the years we've had other tipsters asking why they're not mentioned on 'The Morning Line'," says Channel 4's John McCririck. "It's simply because Pricewise is the only one who moves the market. That's why security around Mel and Tom's tips has to be so tight. Getting that information early is invaluable because people know it's going to shorten."

McCririck believes that the column's profile has been crucial to its survival. "The brand name is a huge advantage for Pricewise," he says. "The winners are puffed up by the *Post* – rightly so – and people are always shouting and screaming about the successes. Then I'll go on the television and say a winner had been tipped up by Pricewise, which only makes it worse! It is perceived as a success, which is why it can survive long losing runs. I'm sure it's had runs of around 40 losers and we publicise that fact on Channel 4. Of course, you can understand why that is, because the hardest races are chosen for Pricewise and it's very rare that they'll tip a favourite. But there's no sycophancy on Channel 4's part. We talk about Pricewise because of its influence on the market but we're not afraid to point out when it has a bad run."

While McCririck was an early convert to Pricewise, *The Sporting Life* was slow to respond to its rival's increasingly prominent new column. "They were quite late in to the game," says Collier. "I think they missed a trick because the Pricewise idea – the word Pricewise, even – was really beginning to establish itself but the *Life* didn't seem to recognise that. I'm not sure why not, whether it was an editorial decision or whether there were other commercial pressures, but they certainly missed a trick."

It wasn't until October 1993 when *The Sporting Life* launched its response to Pricewise, Mark Winstanley's Beat the Book column. According to James Lambie's history of the paper, *The Story Of Your Life*, the column had "one purpose in mind – 'to take the bookies' trousers down as often as possible'." Winstanley blasted out of the blocks: his first selection was Aahsaylad, a 14-1 winner of the Cesarewitch, and he followed up two weeks later by tipping Triple Witching, who was backed from 20-1 in to 17-2, to win the Tote Silver Trophy Handicap Hurdle at Chepstow.

"Mark Winstanley started off really well," Collier recalls. "By then, though, Pricewise had already made its name. I didn't know Mark personally but there was definitely a rivalry running through the two papers because it was a small market and the *Post* had been gradually chipping away at the *Life*'s circulation lead. So there was a bit of extra pressure from Mark but I always felt that the *Life* was too slow to react to Pricewise."

Alan Byrne, having worked as news editor, editor, chief executive and editor-in-chief of the *Racing Post*, is uniquely qualified to discuss the commercial significance of Pricewise's growth. "I think when Mel first took the job, Channel 4 Racing was also establishing itself and doing lots of midweek days. The bookmakers were pricing up more races than ever before and the volume of racing was increasing. Pricewise started before all-weather racing – that didn't come in until 1989 – so I suspect if you looked at the total fixtures in the late 1980s, there might have been 750 or 800 per year as opposed to 1,500 nowadays.

"So there was more racing, for a start, and bookmakers were getting better at trading them and were offering more early prices. The volume of racing that came into the Pricewise domain was increasing. But we wouldn't have wanted to be doing Pricewise every day because it would lose some of its impact. It might have been too much to have it in the paper every day.

"From a commercial point of view, I think the *Racing Post* has enjoyed a lot of reflected glory from Pricewise. If you're in the business of racing newspapers and your selling point is 'we do the homework for you and we're offering our expertise on horse racing' then to have a flagship column that talks the talk and walks the walk – and actually achieves things – is fantastic.

"It has done a lot for the *Racing Post*'s credibility and importance in the racing and betting communities. Pricewise is there as the flagship column with a record of success and an impact on the market that has been consistent throughout the years. Probably if you asked a thousand people at the racecourse or in betting shops for something that they associate with the *Racing Post*, Pricewise would be one of the most popular answers."

Pricewise's growth under Mel Collier was partly due to a regular supply of winners but it also relied on the support of bookmakers and television. "It was always very much tied in with the terrestrial TV races," Collier says. "I'd know the TV racing on the Friday and I'd ring round the bookies to find out which races they were pricing up in advance. I'd have a general idea of the kind of races they'd bet on – they were always prepared to price up big sprint handicaps and handicap chases but they were less keen on the stakes races. Obviously, they might not want to bet on a race if there was a big question mark over whether the favourite or second-favourite would run, or if there were major concerns about the ground.

"I'd have a ring round and they'll tell me 'we're going to do these three races tomorrow' and I'd start working away at those. I'd have done some preparatory work, looking at the draw, the pace, the form, and perhaps coming up with a shortlist. The form was almost a given because everyone had access to it so I'd be looking more for things that people might have missed about a particular horse. I might think the fact that it's not wearing blinkers could make a massive difference. I often liked taking on horses running under a penalty. You know, they're due to go up 12lb but they've only got a 4lb penalty so connections feel obliged to run them again and so often in those cases they'd just blow out completely.

"I'd be thinking in general terms about the race and the prices would start dribbling in at about 4pm. There was always a bit of a game with deadlines because the advertising deadlines were tighter than the editorial deadlines. The bookmakers had to get their adverts in earlier but they could still make changes with me. If there was rain around, Ladbrokes might ring up and shorten up three or four soft-ground horses, for example.

"Once I'd got the whole grid – all the prices from a dozen or so bookmakers – I could start looking for discrepancies. Immediately I'd see, for instance, that Coral were three points bigger than everybody else about a horse and maybe I'd remember that they had an 'in' to that particular stable. Or I'd look at the Ladbrokes prices and see they were expecting it to be a draw-type race. Early on, in Mark's day, there would be massive variation in the prices because each individual bookmaker would be compiling his odds pretty much in isolation, which is why Mark sometimes had under 100-per-cent books. But bookies are very clever – they weren't going to carry on doing 90-per-cent books for long – so by the time I started doing Pricewise the prices would have already been through a couple of filters. The firms got the industry tissue, then their own men would make a few changes, and once they got down to me there were far fewer obvious ricks.

"I'd have the full table of prices through by about 6pm. I liked to have a look at the other newspaper tipsters' selections. There were two or three who I really respected and 80 per cent of the time I'd be able to see their reasoning although sometimes I didn't know why the hell they had tipped something! Eventually, I'd come to a conclusion. Sometimes I'd be almost certain all day that I was going to tip a particular horse but the prices would be a real disappointment. If I was expecting 8-1 and it came over at 4-1, I'd just have to start again, which is a good thing in general. I've missed winners doing that but I've also found some big winners that I wouldn't have found otherwise.

"There was always tension between the production staff, who wanted to get the paper off to the printers, and the editorial side. There was pressure from the subs too. They'd be asking 'what's the headline going to be?' and I'd have to tell them 'I don't know, I haven't seen all the prices yet' or 'I just want to watch the 5.30 at Newmarket because it might show that there's a bias favouring the far side.' Sometimes it was a real struggle, in extreme circumstances with the deadline looming. I remember a couple of Lincolns on heavy ground when if I thought there was a draw bias I'd just end up looking at the top six on that rail or the top six on the other rail, seeing what goes on soft ground, what acts in big fields, and suddenly this horse would appear at 28-1 and that would be the tip."

The relationship between Pricewise and the bookmakers is a complex one. The bookies were never likely to warm to a column which sought to publicise – and exploit – their mistakes. However, as its influence grew stronger, firms had to recognise the value to their business of appearing in the Pricewise grids and accommodating the column's followers.

"I did build up an interesting relationship with the odds compilers," says Collier. "Their game was to try and talk me into tipping a horse that they fancied and were therefore short about. They didn't want to have the liability guys on their cases, saying 'you've tipped the Pricewise horse again – why are we 14-1 about this one?' So some of the compilers – Coral and Tote, in particular – would be keen for a chat whereas Ladbrokes would just send the prices over through their PR department. I'd never tell the compilers what I was tipping, obviously, but there was an element of cloak-and-dagger about it. If we were talking about a race, I'd often put a conventional view to them – 'that's a seven-furlong horse, really, isn't it?' – and they'd agree enthusiastically but I'd be thinking 'Oh no it isn't!' So there was a bit of bluff and double-bluff going on, which just added another layer of interest.

"You'd get to know which firms were particularly hot on certain trainers and jockeys but sometimes they could be too close to them. I remember tipping a winner at Cheltenham despite the fact that somebody had told me the trainer didn't fancy it. And after it had won at a big price, somebody else told me that Ladbrokes had phoned the trainer and said 'look, we've seen a lot of money for this – what do you think?' And he'd told them 'no, we don't fancy it.' So you can lose the objective overview of a race if you're too close to things like that.

"Over the years I was accused of being in the pocket of, or colluding with, various bookmakers – Ladbrokes was the most popular among the conspiracy theorists – so it was particularly satisfying to tip a big winner with the Magic Sign. When Heidi won the Great Yorkshire Chase, Ladbrokes were biggest priced at 33-1 in the morning, which silenced those conspiracy theorists for a while."

Despite protests from the tinfoil hat brigade, any kind of skulduggery or collusion with bookmakers was extremely unlikely. As Collier says, the high profile of Pricewise meant that "you'd be aware that the eyes of the world were on you. Considering the potential for fraud and jiggery-pokery, I was – and I'm sure Tom is – very strict about keeping the tipping side separate from my own betting. If I fancied something in a fully open ante-post race like the Cambridgeshire then I might ask someone to put a bet on for me. I wouldn't get on under my own name because that's a bit of a clue for the bookies, isn't it? But I wouldn't have any problems with asking a friend to get on for me in that sort of race.

"When it came to the normal Saturday Pricewise races, though, the gun would go off at 9am or 9.30am and I'd be there getting knocked back along with everybody else. I'd be ringing AR Dennis and they'd be knocking me back, I'd be ringing Hills and they'd be knocking me back, so I felt the same frustration as everybody else. I know some journalists could be a bit cosy with the bookies and they'd be allowed to get on at mates' rates. But because Pricewise was so public, I don't think there was ever the opportunity for that sort of thing – and anyway, it's not in my nature or Tom's nature to do that. It's not as if we're MPs or bankers!"

Pricewise's longevity is testament to the integrity of its tipsters. They have to handle the pressure of expectations and maintain their equilibrium during long losing runs but they also enjoy enormous job satisfaction. Collier regarded each race as a puzzle and says that, when the puzzle was solved, "It was fantastic. It was the clenched fist in front of the TV. That's the pay-off emotionally – the real sense of 'yes, I called that one right' or 'I knew that rail was dead.' And there's also the nerdy bean-counting side of it, when you look through the records and see that you've made 16 per cent profit on turnover, or whatever it might be, that year. So there's the immediate thrill of watching the race and the longer-term satisfaction too.

"The ego was never really a factor for me, though, partly because I didn't actually go racing very often. I think Channel 4 once put me on the shortlist for their Racing Personality of the Year. So there was Frankie Dettori and whoever else and then 'who's that? Oh, that's me!' Obviously, I wasn't going to beat Frankie and I was never in it for the personal glory but I didn't mind increasing the profile of tipsters and analysts. I felt that tipsters in general were undervalued. That was a bugbear of mine. If you're analysing the stock market, then you're a whizz-kid superstar whereas if you're analysing a horse race, you're a dead-beat punter. But it's the same sort of discipline, basically, so I was always happy if I could increase the legitimacy of tipsters."

Although Collier's mantelpiece was never graced by Channel 4's Racing Personality of the Year award, his tipping record throughout the 1990s and early 2000s boosted Pricewise's credibility enormously. He recorded a profit every year from 1993 to 2001, making 52 per cent profit on turnover in 1995 and a whopping 69 per cent in 2000. Hits such as Cool Dawn in the Cheltenham Gold Cup and Papillon in the Grand National are documented in greater detail in Chapter Eight but Collier's winners also included Glencloud (25-1) in the Ladbroke Handicap Hurdle at Leopardstown in 1993, Ochos Rios (33-1) in a 27-runner handicap at York in 1996, Toby Balding's Star Precision (25-1) at York in 1999, and Beau (25-1) at Doncaster in 2000. Unlike his successor Segal, he kept meticulous records and enjoyed using the *Racing Post*'s staking plan which, nowadays, ranges from one point for a speculative punt up to ten points for maximum-bet material.

"I can understand why Tom doesn't really use the points system," Collier says. "He'll usually just have one point win on his selections. The thing in favour of the points is that it shows the reader the strength of your enthusiasm about a tip. Equally, though, is it realistic to expect to get four points on with most bookies, or at least to get them on at the price quoted in the paper? I think Hugh Taylor on the At The Races website is very good these days but he started with a wide points range – one to six, perhaps

– which has gradually been squeezed. Now he'll mostly put up one- and two-point tips. I don't know whether that's psychological on the part of the tipsters. They've already chosen their tip and they don't want to make yet another decision. Should they put two points or three points on it? Should they have one point win and three points place or two points each-way? It's another layer of complexity or annoyance."

In any case, according to Paul Kealy all that agonising over staking plans may well be in vain. "I remember Mel having, I think, seven points on She's Our Mare to win the Cambridgeshire in 1999," Kealy says. "But the headline was about one of his other selections, so that one was smashed up early on and the price about She's Our Mare, the really strong tip, held for a bit longer. That showed me that headlines will always grab the readers more than staking plans do!"

The points system did used to draw criticism from some quarters, as Collier admits: "I used to get people saying 'your entire year's profit was down to a four-point tip on that 33-1 shot.' But that's the point of Pricewise, in a way, isn't it? I was looking to hit three or four big winners in a year and that's what I did. That approach would feel completely wrong for some people. They can't take the losing runs and they're much happier backing 4-1 shots and getting the comfort blanket of a winner more frequently. Some people are more suited to that emotionally but my mentality has always pushed me towards the big-priced winners rather than grinding out the 6-4 shots. I was never much good at spotting the 7-4 shot that should be 11-8 or 6-4. Percentage-wise, that's quite a big difference but in my head it still looks short. As I said, I was always much better at picking a 12-1 shot that should be 7-1 or 8-1."

The nature of that approach meant there were inevitable periods without a winner. A mathematically-minded friend of Collier's once worked out just how long a losing streak should be expected for a tipster picking a genuine 8-1 chance every week of the year. Collier doesn't recall the exact figure but he admits it was both terrifying and heartening. "I thought 'OK, I'm not doing too badly here'," he says, showing commendable modesty for a man who defied not only the nation's bookmakers but also the laws of probability.

While Mark Coton often felt that he was fighting a lone battle, his successor enjoyed the support of his superiors. "When I was going through a bad run – and obviously you have good runs and bad runs – Alan Byrne would come over and have a word," Collier remembers. "He'd never be critical, he'd just tell me to carry on, that I was doing well, that sort of thing. And I never got too wound up over the bad runs because I could only do my best. That's what I did and sometimes it worked and sometimes it didn't. Sometimes I'd tip a 16-1 shot that finished third and one at 8-1 that was beaten a short head and suddenly the losing run would have built up to 15 or 20. You don't want to do that – it's not your plan and you're doing the same stuff you've always done but it just hasn't happened in that particular month. So you have to have an equitable temperament. It's a difficult business. If you're quite frail psychologically, it can certainly mess with you. You don't really need the outside pressure because you put such immense pressure on yourself.

"The difficult thing is becoming established and getting people to believe in you. Once that happens, if you tip ten losers in a row, people still believe your 11th tip is going to win – and often it does. By the time I felt established in the job, Alan or somebody might tell me in a jokey way about a letter from some bloke saying that I'm rubbish, that he could tip 57 straight winners – which people think they can do! But that was all part of the very public nature of Pricewise. More than any other tipster, people discuss or slag off or praise the Pricewise selection and that's something that you just have to deal with. I think that public side of it ensured that I gave it 100 per cent. It's not like turning up for work and keeping your head down and getting through the day – it's a very public thing. You make sure that you do a 100-per-cent job and don't miss anything if you can possibly help it. I think that focus is a big part of Pricewise's success.

"A friend of mine, Simon Stanley, went through the card on his very first day as a Spotlight writer because he felt the whole world was watching. The adrenaline was pumping and he did a fantastic job – I doubt if he ever went through the card again after that! So the public side of the job can be helpful. There were moments when I was being criticised and moments when I was being praised up but you've got to treat those two imposters just the same."

Alan Byrne is unequivocal about what Collier calls 'the public side of the job'. "It is the highest-profile job in tipping," Byrne says. "There isn't another column that has the same influence. That does bring a big responsibility with it so you can't just be a guesser. Happily none of the people who have been entrusted with Pricewise have been guessers – quite the opposite, they've had a methodical and rigorous approach which has paid off. The readers of the *Racing Post* have probably been fortunate in that Mark, Mel and Tom have all been conscious of the responsibility they have as custodians of Pricewise. Between them, they've established a very important service and a very important brand."

Collier's sensational sequence of profitable years as Pricewise had inevitably attracted attention. "I'd had several offers to deal private tips and I'd been doing Pricewise for a few years so I felt I was at the top of my share price, if you like. I'd spoken to Henry Rix, whose Betting Bureau column had been as big as Pricewise in its day, and he'd gone down the private route and done well out of it and I thought 'it's now or never.' It was a really emotional decision to leave. The *Post* had been very good to me so I didn't want to stitch them up. But financially, for myself and my family, it was the right thing to do.

"Private tipping brings a different kind of pressure because it's so direct. It's not for the ten-quid punter in the betting shop, it's for real, hardcore gamblers. I think Pricewise is designed for a certain type of punter – if you're super clued-up and looking to get two grand on then it's not for you. But I didn't change my tipping style because I was known for doing Pricewise and I was still tipping in the bigger meetings so I just tried to replicate what I'd been doing for all those years."

Collier's huge contribution to Pricewise wasn't just about big-priced winners and profitable seasons – he also nominated Tom Segal as his successor. "Get this on record," he demands with a grin. "When Alan Byrne asked who I'd choose to replace me, I recommended Tom. I don't know to what extent it's tied to one person, though – I was successful at it, Tom's been successful at it and I'm sure whoever replaces Tom in the long term will be equally successful."

He is well aware of the need for Pricewise to adapt to the ever-changing betting world. "I'm very pleased that it's become so established but in a way we were shooting ourselves in the foot. We were writing about radical new ideas and obviously the bookmakers took that on board. They got to know the kind of tips I liked to do and they started shaving points off them so something I'd definitely have tipped at 12-1 was only 10-1. From a selfish point of view, you never want to give too much away but I think the general punter has been educated a lot over the last 20 years – not just by me, obviously, but by everybody. Before Camelot won the 2,000 Guineas there was a lot of talk about his sire Montjeu never having had a three-year-old Group 1 winner over a mile. Ten years ago the general punter just wouldn't have been involved in that kind of debate.

"In the early days of Pricewise the compiler could make a mistake and you'd seize on it. It's much less likely nowadays that they'll make a rick of those proportions. They're not going to have missed the fact that a horse has run in France or that a different jockey's riding it – there will be a reason why they're offering a price and you can either agree or disagree with that reason. There's been a massive increase in knowledge so you've got to become ten per cent better just to stay in line with everybody else who's getting ten per cent better.

"Just look at the availability of videos on the *Racing Post* website – it's fantastic. I remember Ian Heaney [now managing director of the *Post*'s Digital Division] telling me about ten years ago that we might get to a stage where you could click on a horse's name and see the race. Whereas Andrew Barr, who I also used to work with, had libraries of VHS tapes. I'd sometimes ask him 'could you look up so-and-so's Lingfield run from May 19?' and there'd be a lot of fast-forwarding and rewinding and literally 20 minutes later we'd get to the right race!

"But the information that is hardest to find is usually the most valuable. I've found myself betting more and more on jumps racing because there's more to analyse. When I first started, it was hard to find the basics – a horse's lifetime form, stuff like that – but now everybody's got access to that so I think the value has shifted to the little individual quirks of certain horses. Lots of horses, especially jumpers, display these quirks quite early in their careers. You can see the ones that have trouble jumping or don't want to go in left-handed but often that doesn't seem to be factored into the prices for novice hurdles. There are so many more variables in those kind of races than, say, a two-year-old race on the flat where there are only one or two previous runs to consider for each horse. And because there are more variables, it's far more chaotic; and the more chaotic it is, the more likely the bookmakers are to make a mistake.

"What tends to happen when you're a bit older is that you fall back on things that have served you well over the years. But they might be the things that are overbet now. You go from being anti-establishment, a young Turk, and suddenly you find yourself part of the establishment and it's more difficult. I think the successful older punters are the ones who are honest with themselves and continually re-evaluate their betting strategies. Have I had a good year? Why not? Is a particular trainer that I follow tailing off a bit? Look at Henry Cecil, for example – a fantastic trainer, absolutely at the pinnacle, then a big dip, and now back at the top again. So I think it is becoming more difficult although I don't know whether that's because I'm getting older and life in general is more difficult! But that's part of the reason why I still love working on the puzzle of a race – the puzzle is always changing, the pieces are always shifting shapes."

"THE TOMINATOR"

Tom Segal's golden run of 2005 is documented by the Racing Post. The winning sequence would continue with Tax Free's victory on August 27.

THE SCOURGE OF BRITAIN'S bookmakers lives in the quiet commuter town of Fleet, in Hampshire. He plays a bit of golf and works from a small office within earshot of his children's Lego-strewn playroom. Tom Segal is an affable, sports-obsessed father-of-two, who is happier discussing the

Tom Segal took over as Pricewise in the summer of 2001 after Mel Collier's departure

form of Reading FC or the England cricket team rather than big-priced winners and betting coups. It is hard to picture the self-effacing Segal as a "scourge" of anything, really, but there is no denying the impact that he has made on the betting industry since inheriting the Pricewise mantle in the summer of 2001.

Like his predecessor Mel Collier, Segal has no close family ties to racing. His interest in the sport was a mere accident of birth; a quirk of fate that battered bookmakers have been regretting for more than a decade. "I was born in Esher, right on Sandown Park," Segal explains. "My parents aren't really racing fans but a few of their friends were so they'd take me to Gold Cups and Eclipses. That's what you do when you're in Esher. There's a cinema, good earth, the racecourse and not much else."

After school in Surrey and an economics degree at Cardiff University, Segal might have been expected to pursue one of the more traditional financial professions. A brief spell working for a shipbroking firm in London did little to inspire the young graduate and soon he started on his meandering path to the Pricewise hot seat. "I used to go racing and I liked having a bet but I'd never had a plan to work in the industry," he says. "I was one of those blokes who wasn't cut out for working in the City. I just couldn't stand it. I hated every minute of it. So I got a job at Weatherbys in Wellingborough for a couple of years, compiling data for Raceform. When that moved to Compton, I didn't go with it. I came back home, wrote to the *Racing Post* and Ian Heaney gave me a job on the data desk."

Perhaps unsurprisingly, Segal felt more at home in the *Racing Post*'s Raynes Park offices than he had done in the Square Mile. Mel Collier remembers that staff at the *Post* still regarded themselves as "the upstarts" in relation to the long-established *Sporting Life*. As a newly-recruited data compiler, Segal relished that atmosphere. "It was a small paper trying to make its way so there was a real sense of community," he says. "When I joined it had been going for four or five years but there was still the feeling that you were fighting for a cause – you had to get this thing up and running. We had a good little group on our desk and basically we'd work our balls off! We'd regularly be there until midnight but it was good fun. You don't get many jobs where you can go in and enjoy yourself with the racing on the telly. It's not like working in a bank, is it?"

The opportunity to discuss racing with like-minded enthusiasts was a perk of the job as far as Segal was concerned. "I like talking about horse racing and Emily Weber liked talking about horse racing and Henry Rix liked talking about horse racing," he recalls. "So I used to sit around at lunch chatting with them and they must have thought that I sort of knew what I was talking about because Emily suggested that I try doing some Spotlights."

Writing Spotlight verdicts was Segal's first experience of the public nature of tipping. "It was difficult to begin with," he admits. "Someone says to you 'write a Spotlight' and you feel quite nervous about it. It's a totally new discipline and you think the whole world is going to read it so it does feel very important. But you can't dwell on it too much because the main thing is getting the paper out before deadline. The main challenge is time. If I could go back and do it all again with an extra half an hour then I would but, as with anything, the more you do it the less nerve-wracking it seems."

Segal's first piece of advice to aspiring tipsters and punters is to watch as many races as possible. However, that wasn't always easy in the days of VHS: "I used to video Channel 4 or BBC races and watch them again and again and again," he says. "But I'd still find doing Spotlights for the smaller races really hard. Obviously, I didn't know the horses as well as I knew the runners in big races and my methodology would always be to watch the races so in the old days, struggling with just three lines of form, it was tough. What's written down on paper doesn't give you any idea about what actually happened during a race. It's a very personal thing, though – Emily, for example, loved doing the smaller races and I liked the bigger races. Over the years it evolved so that I ended up doing the kind of races I was best at."

That instinctive feel for the big races made Segal a strong candidate to deputise as Pricewise when Mel Collier was away. The super-sub was well aware of the responsibility that came with what was, by then, the *Racing Post*'s flagship tipping column. "For a start, Mel was really conscientious and really good," he says. "I didn't want to let him down, or let down Alan Byrne and Emily and all the other people who had given me the chance. So I was aware of the tradition and the prestige of Pricewise but the pressure was mainly internal – you just want to do the best in anything you do."

Segal appreciated his colleagues' support but tipsters cannot survive on good will alone. While he was still Collier's deputy, he tipped a couple of big-priced winners which helped to settle the nerves and boost his credibility with the column's readers. "There was one called Sharoura that won a sprint handicap at Yarmouth at 25-1," he recalls fondly. "I was still a bit green back then, happily throwing points around willy-nilly. I think Sharoura was a four- or a five-point tip so when it won it took the pressure off immediately. I was suddenly 100 points in profit, which is what people judge you on, even though it's a load of nonsense really. You should only be judged on your last tip, I think, although when you're having a lean spell it's nice to be able to say 'hang on, I did actually have four points on that 25-1 winner not so long ago...'"

Sharoura's victory came in September 1999. The previous November, Segal had been "happily throwing" eight points on Suny Bay to win the Edward Hanmer Memorial Chase at Haydock. It was a selection that disregarded popular opinion at the *Racing Post* – "everyone in the office fancied See More Business" – but, not for the last time, Segal was proved right. The opening sentence of that day's column is a reminder of how the logistics of the job have changed during his time as Pricewise: "I got a bit of a shock when the fax came through with the prices for today's Showcase race as, much to my surprise, last year's winner Suny Bay was only fourth favourite for this season's renewal." The fax machine and the Showcase handicaps are historical footnotes now but the next line of the preview would have been just as relevant to Mark Coton in 1987 or Tom Segal in 2012: "I'm convinced he will start favourite at around 5-2 so the advice is to snap up the 4-1 with Coral and Surrey." Suny Bay, sent off as 2-1 favourite, beat Escartefigue by five lengths with See More Business back in fourth.

Although the Pricewise column had a clear ethos, set out by Mark Coton, Segal never felt constrained by the role. "I had my approach, my style, and Mel had a totally different approach," he says. "He was far more figures-orientated, more regimented, and he'd go through a race with a fine toothcomb, looking at each and every runner. I tend to look at a race and immediately whittle it down to four or five horses, then muck around with them for the rest of the day until it's time to tip one. But I never felt pressure to change that approach or to tailor it to Pricewise. You can only do what works for your individual personality."

Value is the key of the Pricewise operation although Segal concedes that it can be a murky area. "Value is a very difficult thing to define," he says. "I think you can get a feeling about whether or not a horse is going to be backed on the day. Look at the quotes from the jockey, or the trainer form, or the tipsters' selection box and you'll get a sense of whether it's well fancied and, therefore, whether this particular 6-1 shot is a good 6-1 shot or not. I think Mark Coton says that value is the most expensive word in betting and he's quite right, in a way. You're much better off tipping a

7-4 winner than a 6-1 loser. But at the same time it's obvious that value – getting the "right" price – is the key. You don't want to be backing horses that are a shorter price than they should be. It's like going shopping and buying something for a tenner when it's only four quid in the shop next door. You just shouldn't do it."

Segal is revered by punters for his knack of finding winners at big prices. That trend is partly a reflection of his own tipping style but it is also due to the type of races that Pricewise covers. "Opposing favourites is part and parcel of the Pricewise job," he explains. "Don't get me wrong, if there's a favourite that I think should be 7-4 and it's 5-1, I'm not averse to tipping it – of course not. But often I'll be tipping on a 20-runner handicap and in those kind of races the 5-1 favourite isn't normally the one you're going to go for.

"I'm a pretty laid-back character. I wouldn't be the type to spend ten hours on a race, trawling through the formbook. As Pricewise, because I'm doing the best races, with horses that I know well, I'm immediately able to get down to those four or five that I'd feel confident tipping. Obviously, they might not win – they might be totally the wrong four or five, in fact – but they're the ones that suit my style of tipping. The prices are the key, though. If they come over and one of the horses I've picked is half the price I expected it to be, that one will be off the list. It might well still win but I can't be sure that it's the right tip. There's a massive difference between tipping and betting. They're two totally different games.

"I'm not a massive punter by any stretch of the imagination. Punting has never been that high on my agenda. I like betting and I back 90 per cent of the horses I tip but I wouldn't be having thousands of pounds on – it's just a bit of fun. I'm much better at tipping than I am at betting and the main pleasure I get out of my job is trying to solve the puzzle. I like the structure of the job too. I get to watch racing in an environment that suits my temperament and hopefully I can find a few winners for people. But the punting, the betting, is very much a sideline."

Mel Collier was always keen to canvass a wide selection of opinions, asking colleagues for their thoughts on the draw, pace, form and trends before coming to a conclusion about a race. In contrast, Segal prefers to work it out on his own and seems a little wary of any external factors that might contaminate his personal analysis. "It wasn't my choice to work from home," he says. "It was a space thing. The paper's staff had got so big by the time it moved to Canary Wharf that there wasn't room for everybody. But it's worked out well because I'm very conscious of not being influenced by anybody else. I'm conscious of just letting it be me making the decisions. When you're sitting up in the *Racing Post* office you have everybody coming along saying 'what do you fancy?' and 'why are you going for that one? I fancy this.' You'd have to be Superman not to have those people's voices invading your consciousness. Whereas if you can stay out of the way, stay in your own bubble, then you live and die by your own decisions. If you get it right then you've done well; if you get it wrong then it's nobody else's fault."

There is nothing of the prima donna about this approach. It is more about self-reliance and staying sane in a high-pressure job. The young Segal fretted that the whole world would be reading his early Spotlight verdicts; now, as Pricewise, the whole racing world really does watch his every move. The *Racing Post*'s associate editor Francis Kelly admiringly refers to "Tom's laissez-faire attitude – he'll go off to watch a Reading match on a Saturday afternoon when the entire racing industry is hanging on one of his tips!" Alan Byrne, the *Racing Post*'s chief executive and editor-in-chief isn't convinced, however. "Tom is always playing down the degree to which he works at it," he says "but, like Mark and Mel before him, he approaches his racing with a great rigour."

Segal often talks about the importance of an individual's temperament when it comes to tipping and betting. He revealed his own personality traits in a *Racing Post* interview with Peter Thomas in February 2012: "I'm inherently incredibly lazy. I drive a Skoda when everybody says I should drive a Mercedes and the last time I went to the cinema I nodded off halfway through the film." It's not an attitude that would serve Segal well on 'The Apprentice' but it does help him remain level-headed whether his tips are winning or losing.

"I personally take the pressure off myself quite well," he says. "I've never felt that other tipsters are rivals, as such. We'd get *The Sporting Life* in the office and see what they'd gone for – I'm sure the guys there were excellent tipsters – but I can only do what I do. I'm sure there are millions of guys out there who are better tipsters than me but I'm the one who's got the Pricewise job and I'm trying to do it the best I can. Occasionally you get people moaning, saying 'he's had 40 losers in a row' or whatever, but most people who follow the tips are just having a bit of fun. That's what Pricewise is about. You go into the betting shop and you have your fiver on at 20-1. If it wins, great; if it doesn't, don't worry – it's just a horse race."

Confidence is crucial for any tipster and Segal has always been grateful to the support network that he enjoys at the *Racing Post*. "When I first got the Pricewise job on a full-time basis, I remember Alan Byrne calling me into his office," he says. "He said to me, 'Look, I don't care how you do – you can have 50 straight losers as long as I feel you're putting the effort in, trying your hardest and not guessing.' I can't stress enough how important it was to hear that. It's all you can ask for, isn't it?"

Byrne is fully aware of the pressure of the job. "In the good times it's fantastic but in the bad times there's a lot of heat," he says. "As Tom has said to me, if you're meeting your mates and they're all averting their gaze, you know you're on a bad run. As editor I used to get letters saying 'why do you make such a fuss about Pricewise – he's rubbish, he couldn't tip excrement off a shovel.' Then, of course, the column would have a blinding run.

"I think the editors of the paper have always been quite responsible. If Pricewise has had a long losing run and then has a few winners to start balancing the books, nobody trumpets it or shouts about it until we're back to the point where the people who follow the column are quids in again."

Segal keeps himself detached from the hysteria that often surrounds Pricewise. The *Racing Post*'s editorial staff are eager to flag up winners in the next day's paper. These stories tend to be based around bookmakers' reactions as the firms' PR departments, like elderly hypochondriacs, each claim that fate has dealt them the cruellest hand. Pricewise tips are analysed, debated, praised and pilloried on the comments section of the *Post*'s website and, increasingly, on Twitter. Over on the Betfair forum, contributors cheerily accuse Segal of everything from collusion with the bookmakers to witchcraft. Mel Collier was well aware of the publicity that Pricewise could bring – he appeared on Channel 4's 'The Morning Line' once, after prolonged badgering from his bosses at the *Post* – but he doesn't envy Segal's profile. "I'd much rather crawl back under a rock, if at all possible," Collier admits.

If Segal has indeed attained celebrity status in racing – however reluctantly – then he has only himself to blame. An extraordinary run of winning tips in 2005, between June 25 and August 27, brought Pricewise to wider prominence. He was already renowned within the racing industry after picking Monty's Pass in the 2003 Grand National and enjoying a golden Friday at Royal Ascot the same year when he rattled in winners at 16-1, 6-1 and 33-1 in the space of an hour and a half. But the summer of 2005 is one that Pricewise followers look back on with the hazy fondness of hippies recalling the Summer of Love.

Segal bashfully refers to those ten consecutive winning Saturdays as "my good run". No doubt punters – and bookmakers, in particular – refer to the sequence in rather more colourful terms. From Sergeant Cecil in the Northumberland Plate to Tax Free, tipped at 7-2 for the William Hill Trophy at York and sent off a bullish 9-4 favourite, everything seemed to fall into place for Pricewise that summer. According to Segal, there is no explanation for the Midas touch – he hadn't started eating kippers for breakfast or wearing lucky underpants, for example. It all just came together.

"All you're doing is trying to tip a few winners and I find it's very cyclical," he says. "You have good runs and bad runs and funnily enough all the good runs seem to come together and all the bad runs seem to come together. They're not interspersed, but that's just the way it happens. Look at how Chelsea won the Champions League [in 2012]. It was unbelievable – those two games against Barcelona and then the final. Gary Neville was talking about fate on Sky Sports, which makes it sound mystical, but it's not mystical – it's luck. There was no coaching, no tactics, it had nothing to do with the players. It was simply down to luck. It was just that Lionel Messi missed a penalty in the semi-final and Arjen Robben missed one in the final.

"That's what happens with tipping. You go through periods when you're not doing anything differently in terms of looking at the races but you end up making the right decision more often than not. Maybe it's got something to do with confidence because when you're on a bad run, making those decisions becomes more difficult. You either start playing it safe, being more cautious, or you think 'I've got to hit one out of the park' and go looking for a spectacular winner.

"There was a winner at Newmarket recently called Mince. It was around

6-1 in the morning and if anyone had phoned me up I'd have said, without a doubt, that the horse was going to win. Did I tip it? No, because it was 6-1 in a 20-runner handicap so I didn't really feel it was the one for me. But when you're having a good run you can tick them off automatically – that's the one, that's the one. It's just a clarity of thought that comes with confidence. And, when you're not confident, everything gets that little bit more convoluted."

Segal discussed this "clarity of thought" in an interview with *The Guardian*'s Stephen Moss on September 9, 2005. "During these ten weeks, I found myself tipping horses I didn't think I would ever tip and they were winning," he told Moss. "Take Courageous Duke at Haydock. He hadn't won for two or three years and normally I don't like tipping horses like that. But the race had fallen apart for him; everything had come right and I was able to see that. You sometimes get a moment of clarity that hits you between the eyes."

There was no disguising Segal's confidence after nine profitable Saturdays in a row. His tenth preview, on August 27, began: "There are not many places in the world where you can earn three and a half times your money for about a minute's work. You can at York this afternoon – and it'll be tax free!" And, as was so often the case for Pricewise horses in the summer of 2005, everything went right for Tax Free. The Dandy Nicholls sprinter held on to win by a neck from Intrepid Jack, whose jockey Steve Drowne dropped his whip in the closing stages of the race. John McCririck described it as "a monumental gamble" and there was an inevitable paean to Pricewise on the front page of the following day's *Racing Post*. "1, 2, 3, 4, 5, 6, 7, 8, 9, 10... Counted Out!" bellowed the headline while the sub-deck gloated: "Bookies on canvas as Tax Free continues Pricewise's glorious Saturday run."

Bookmakers' spokesmen came to praise Segal, albeit through gritted teeth. After Ashkal Way – advised at 13-2 in the morning and smashed in to 2-1 favouritism by the off – gave Pricewise a ninth winning Saturday on the spin, Neal Wilkins of Victor Chandler said: "Tom has such a large following now and we've never seen a tipster with a run like this before. What he's done this summer is amazing." Coral's Simon Clare echoed that view, declaring: "This is a momentous achievement by Tom. The bookies have been battered over the last nine weeks and the fact that managing directors of multi-million pound betting companies wake up on Saturday morning and the first thing they think about is Tom Segal puts it into perspective." Ladbrokes spokesman Balthazar Fabricius turned to the world of bloodstock for a fitting tribute to Pricewise: "He's the Sadler's Wells of tipping – he produces the goods time and time again."

Clare now admits that "Tom's golden run of 2005 was a nightmare from a PR perspective because we'd have to come up with a different pithy line for the *Racing Post* each week. By week seven or eight of his run we'd exhausted all the clichés and it was a real struggle to come up with the most original PR response." After Ashkal Way's victory, Wilkins bemoaned the fact that "for the ninth Saturday running it's boiled lino for dinner for the bookie chaps. Never mind meat – we can't afford the veg any more." His opposite number at Hills, David Hood, said: "It's a phenomenal run and it just keeps rolling on. We all hit a purple patch but Tom's gone through every colour of the rainbow."

The bookies even priced up some Segal-themed specials, none of which would have satisfied the strict Pricewise criteria for a 'value' bet. Coral made the tipster just 66-1 to be named BBC Sports Personality of the Year – the Beeb's viewers, inexplicably, voted for a top three of Andrew Flintoff, Ellen MacArthur and Steven Gerrard instead – while Paddy Power offered a slightly menacing 10-1 about him being kidnapped by a bookie. Power also went 66-1 about Segal giving up tipping to become a psychic, 200-1 about him presenting a new series of the game-show 'The Price Is Right' and 250-1 about him batting at No. 11 for England in the decisive fifth Ashes Test against Australia at The Oval.

Behind the PR bluster and the novelty bets, however, Pricewise's run had inflicted some serious damage on the bookmakers. The admission from William Hill's chief executive David Harding that the company's profits had been badly hit by Segal's tipping was gleefully reported on the financial pages of broadsheet and tabloid newspapers. On September 6, *The Guardian* explained to its readers that "Mr Segal's sustained run, which came to an end this weekend, captured the imagination of many punters, leading to dramatic swings in prices each week after his predictions were published." *The Daily Telegraph* described the sequence of winning Saturdays as "a stupendous run" while the *Daily Mirror* headlined its story "William Hell!"

The *Racing Post* greeted Harding's announcement to Hills's shareholders with a mischievous front page featuring a one-word headline – "Sorry!" – and the sub-deck "What can we say? We're full of remorse as the world's leading tipster makes a dent in the bookmakers' half-year results." Segal remembers the publicity surrounding that summer as "surreal" and even at the time he was keen to downplay his achievement. "Luck always plays a part and it helped that the weather was very consistent," he said in his interview with *The Guardian*. "When you're tipping horses the day before a race, all your calculations go out the window if it pisses down – forgive the language."

The evolution of Pricewise under Collier and Segal changed the character of the column, not least because it was now a full-time – and a high-profile – position. Mark Coton points out that: "My job was always on the production team. Mel's job was doing Pricewise and it's the same for Tom now. You feel a bit protective of your own baby in a way but, when you hand it over to somebody else, it's their right to take it on. Mel's approach was radically different to mine – he has a mathematic, scientific kind of mind – and, in turn, Tom's approach is very different to Mel's.

"I think Pricewise changed from a column that was primarily about market dynamics into a showcase for Mel and Tom's exceptional tipping skills. These guys would do what I never used to do. If there was a 30-runner handicap, I used to put a pencil through it – I'm not betting in that field, that's not my sort of race. My sort of race was when there were a dozen runners and I was looking for one that would shorten from 6-1 in to 7-2 because that's the one people wanted. I think now there's an expectation with Pricewise that you're going to give 25-1 or 28-1 winners every week."

While Coton's objective for Pricewise was to anticipate market moves, Segal's tips now create those moves. Coton hoped to identify the horses that would shorten in the betting but today's Pricewise selections are backed off the boards purely because they are Pricewise selections. Even bookmakers who are a couple of points shorter than the best morning price struggle to avoid substantial liabilities on a big-race tip because, as John McCririck says, "People know it's going to shorten." Peter Thomas summed up the attitude of Pricewise followers in his *Racing Post* column on September 5, 2005. "For punters, the conundrum of what to do with Tom Segal's selections was solved a long time ago," wrote Thomas. "If you can't get all you want on at 10-1, have the rest at 6-1. In fact, keep playing at any price until the cashpoint won't give you any more betting vouchers."

Pricewise has been forced to evolve because the bookmakers' ricks on which it fed have become so scarce. Francis Kelly describes the way in which the column has had to move with the times: "Pricewise wasn't supposed to be subject to the writer's whim – it was a vehicle for pulling out good-value prices. You needed your own feel for the game, of course, but if the prices came over and a horse was 10-1 across the board and 16-1 with one firm then that had to be the Pricewise tip. You'd see the big discrepancies and then pounce on them. That's far more difficult now as the bookmakers are 24:7 operations so the price might have gone by the time you've finished writing your piece on Friday afternoon.

"I think Pricewise has moved more towards opinion under Tom. He's had a couple of shocking losing runs – I remember discussing one of them with Chris Smith when he was editor – but in the last few years he's really cracked it. The number of points' profit is irrelevant, really; it's the percentage profit on turnover that matters. If you think that Alex Bird, the great post-war gambler, aimed to make three per cent profit on turnover and Tom's making 20 per cent on his tips – well, that is an astonishing figure. It may not sound amazing to the man in the street, but it's an astonishing figure."

Considering the mystique that surrounds Pricewise, Segal's working day is disappointingly banal. "I get the runners at about 11am," he says, "then I phone the bookmakers to find out which races they are doing. People think it's me who chooses the races but it's got nothing to do with me – the bookies will tell me which races they're pricing up. I make a note of the races, get an idea of the fields and then I'll go for a walk or a bike ride, or go and pick the kids up. That gives me a couple of hours when I'm not consciously thinking about the make-up of the race. Unconsciously, I'll probably have done some work on it but without actually sitting down and studying it. Then, at about 3pm, I'll have a proper look through the videos on the *Racing Post* website. The prices come through at 4pm and by 4.30pm I'll have the guys in the office ringing up, saying 'come on mate – what are you going to tip?' That's the crucial time, from 4.30pm till 5pm. It's make or break whether or not I'm going to tip the winner. I'll be making my decision based on the prices, the videos I've watched, and the work I've done on the race.

"It's the most frustrating thing in the world when a horse that you've had on the shortlist and ruled out at the last minute wins. The frustration comes from the fact that you've done a lot of work, you've got all the preparation right, your thought process has been right but the answer you've given is totally wrong. And, obviously, all people see is the tip. Getting the right day is another source of frustration. You can have all these selections that finish third and then win next time out. Or there's one like Trumpet Major, the Richard Hannon horse I tipped for the Coventry in 2011. It finished way down the field at Ascot but it came out the next year and finished fourth to Camelot in the 2,000 Guineas, well clear of Power, the horse that won the Coventry. That kind of thing happens regularly – you're on the right lines with a horse but you get the wrong day. And it's frustrating beyond belief when it's a toss-up between two horses and it goes the wrong way. It always happens when you're on a bad run, too, never when you're on a good run. But that's part of the job, you just have to put up with it."

Paul Kealy attributes Segal's longevity to his ability to handle those kind of frustrations. "Tom keeps a level head when he's on a long losing run," Kealy says. "He never thinks he's brilliant when things are going well and he never thinks he's an idiot when it's going badly. He doesn't panic or change his approach just because he's on a bad run. He works very hard – he only seems to have about one week off a year – and he can really hammer the bookies, as he did in that summer of 2005.

"It's hard to pinpoint the secret of his success but I like the way he keeps things simple. He doesn't mind going for something at the top of the weights or just tipping what he thinks is the fastest horse. A lot of punters think the top-weight in a big handicap is automatically exposed but often it's not. I think Tom, like me, is more of a 'feel' punter. He's probably stood the test of time better than any other tipster on the paper."

Segal's enthusiasm for racing is a huge factor in his continuing profitability. Spotting a potential star – whether horse, jockey or trainer – is perhaps his chief motivation. One colleague recalls Segal tipping him a 66-1 each-way shot for the men's singles at Wimbledon in 1997. Like most players of that era, Cedric Pioline was thrashed by Pete Sampras in the final but the little-known Frenchman had provided early proof of Segal's eye for an outsider.

"James Willoughby [former chief correspondent of the *Racing Post*] is a mate of mine and I speak to him on a daily basis about racing or golf or American football," he says. "We'll just be theorising about what makes a good bet or a good selection and what it always comes back to is being the first person to spot that horse, or that golfer, or that team. If I'm sticking with what everyone already knows, then I'm never going to be ahead of the game. But if I spot a horse that everyone else thinks is average but I think will improve, then I'm on the right track. Don't get me wrong, 75 or 80 per cent of the time I'll be wrong and it won't have any improvement but if one in every five provides you with a 16-1 winner or a 20-1 winner then you're laughing.

"That's why I love ante-post betting. The evidence isn't there yet so it gives you a better opportunity to project what might happen in the future. Everyone's in the same boat, looking for potential. Lots of people hate ante-post betting because they don't feel they've got all the clues to the puzzle but I don't want all the clues. I want to be using my intuition, projecting what I think might happen. So I do a lot of ante-post betting and most of it is rubbish but the winners are really satisfying because you feel you're the only one in the world who spotted it. Of course you're not – the trainer and the stable staff and the jockey and the owners know all about it – but it feels like you're the first to know. It's a real buzz to get it right, to spot something that nobody else has seen. Sea The Stars was a big one for me, at 25-1 in the 2,000 Guineas, and also Synchronised, who was a very, very favourite horse of mine. The first time I ever noticed him was when he won a novice chase at Chepstow and I remember thinking immediately 'that will win the Welsh National.' So I tipped him to win the Welsh National the next year and he did."

Segal's respect for the jockey's role is discussed in greater detail in the next chapter and he regards identifying potential stars of the saddle as a major part of his job. "There's an absolutely massive gulf between the best jockeys and the worst ones," he says. "It's obvious, really – if you put a footballer from Accrington Stanley into the Arsenal team, he's not going to be able to perform at that level. In racing, though, people assume that if you put some guy who's been riding at Catterick or wherever, on the Derby favourite then he'll be as good as Ryan Moore. That's nonsense! So jockeys are a big thing for me. I always think that I owe an awful lot to Ruby Walsh because I was one of the first people, certainly in England, to cotton on to him. I could see he was brilliant, just from watching him ride in Ireland. Seven or eight years ago he was getting on horses and not making a difference to their prices but making a massive difference to their chances of winning.

"I've met Ruby once or twice and I've met Tony McCoy and I get the impression that it gives the jockeys an extra fillip of confidence if I've tipped their horse. You know, horse racing is a very small world and there's only one daily racing paper. I'm lucky enough to have the main tipping job in the *Racing Post* and I've tipped a few winners so the jockeys think I know what I'm talking about. They might be completely wrong, of course! But it's like a cricketer going out to bat – if someone tells him 'you're in

Ruby Walsh, who won the Grand National on Papillon for Pricewise followers in 2000

tremendous form, you're going to make runs today' then it gives him a boost. When I tip a horse, I'll obviously be concentrating on its strengths, saying it's in the right race or whatever, so immediately the jockey's going out there thinking that he's on one with a decent chance. And I must have said so often in Pricewise and in my Weekender column that Jamie Spencer's brilliant and Ruby Walsh is God that they're bound to feel a bit of warmth towards me."

The weighing-room's admiration for Segal is confirmed by leading flat jockey Richard Hughes. "As jockeys, we would always respect a fellow as good as Pricewise," Hughes says. "You can't keep getting it right and tipping 25-1 winners without knowing your stuff. He does. Some of the things written in other papers are garbage and there are tipsters you wouldn't look at but that's not the case with Pricewise. What's impressive is that he generally has very good reasons for making his selections. He doesn't just pick a horse because a certain trainer is flying. Sometimes he talks about the best way your horse should be ridden, and while you won't always agree, there will be times when he shows you the best way to beat your dangers. That can be very useful."

Respected by jockeys, revered by punters and feared by bookmakers, Pricewise has become the world's leading tipping service. Mark Coton's original idea, nurtured by the talents of Mel Collier and Tom Segal, is now a cornerstone of British and Irish racing. Despite the changes of the last quarter of a century, Francis Kelly believes that the original Pricewise concept remains untarnished. "I think Mark's original idea is still present in Pricewise today," Kelly says. "It's not about your fancy, it's about comparing the work of those compilers who have priced up an event and then picking out the value. It is difficult to prevent the Pricewise tip from being leaked and Betfair might have muddied the waters a little – they're not in the grids because they have no fixed price – but as long as bookmakers guarantee the price for ordinary punters, the column should remain popular."

Paul Kealy is in no doubt that Pricewise has achieved Coton's primary objective. "I think the concept of value is more widely understood now, which is what Mark was aiming to do at the very start," he says. "Now it seems like absolute common sense. These days anyone who's even a half-serious punter has got accounts with every bookmaker and they're not going to take 8-1 about a horse that's 10-1 elsewhere. You'll still hear people saying there's no point getting the value if you don't have the winner but that's nonsense. If you're getting the value regularly then the winners will come."

"There's no reason why Pricewise shouldn't continue to be a success," John McCririck maintains, "but like anything in life it depends on the people involved. Aircraft are fantastic but if the pilot's drunk at the controls it's not so good. If Tom went – and he won't go on for ever, he must have had good offers from elsewhere – then the *Post* would need to find a replacement who could match his results. The system is based on results."

From Taberna Lord in February 1987 to the dozens of Grand National, Cheltenham Festival and Royal Ascot winners, those results have carved out Pricewise's place in the betting landscape. And those impetuous words from Mark Coton at a job interview in 1986 – "I'm not interested in what won ten years ago, I'm interested in what's going to win tomorrow" – really have changed the face of tipping.

BETTING: THE PRICEWISE WAY

SEEING STARS

Pricewise lands 25-1 knockout blow for bookies as Sea The Stars and trainer John Oxx strike in the 2,000 Guineas
▶▶Pages 2-5

A star is born: Tom Segal tipped Sea The Stars at 25-1 to win the 2,000 Guineas because he had "felt there was something brilliant about him" as a two-year-old.

DESPITE WHAT less scrupulous tipping services may claim, there are no short cuts to profitable punting. Pricewise's Tom Segal is particularly wary of 'golden rules' so the ideas discussed in this chapter should be treated as general guidelines rather than strict regulations.

"My only golden rule of betting would be to make it fun," Segal says. "A lot of people try too hard and are too concerned about their results. They get too excited if they have a winner and they get too down if they have a loser. The whole point of tipping and betting is to have some fun. It's not about whether you win £50m or lose £50m. I always think that the idea of Pricewise is to encourage people to have fun with their betting.

"Hopefully they'll back a few big-priced winners and come out on top at the end of the year. That would be my first key point: make sure it's enjoyable. It's the same with anything in life – if you like swimming, go for a swim. If you don't like it, go and do something else."

Like Mark Coton and Mel Collier before him, Segal's success has largely been based on looking at races from different, unusual angles. His next piece of advice, therefore, should come as no surprise.

BE FLEXIBLE IN YOUR THINKING

"I don't really like sticking to rules," Segal admits. "Like most sports, racing is fluid. It changes all the time so having too many fixed rules has to be a bad thing. Someone might say 'you've got to have a high draw at Newmarket' but then the very next week you won't want a high draw. Or the moment you start backing Michael Stoute's horses, his yard might get the cough. Racing changes every couple of weeks. In the past the jockeys would have stayed on the far side at certain tracks and you knew that was where the race would pan out; now they all come up the middle so the races are unfolding differently these days.

"I understand that people need a structure, they need a way into a race. Mel Collier would probably have had a more fixed way of looking at things than I do, with his ratings and speed figures. That was what he needed and he may have found it hard to approach a race without them. Having a specific way in is a good starting-point but you shouldn't back yourself into a corner by saying 'this is the way I think and that's that.'

"Basically, the key to golden rules is not to have any. Especially since Betfair came along, the market is totally and utterly different from how it used to be. It's not some staid thing that you can impose rules and regulations on – it's incredibly fluid so it's important to think fluidly too."

BET TO YOUR TEMPERAMENT

One of the central tenets of Segal's punting philosophy is that it is impossible to separate the punter from the man. There are many different breeds of successful gamblers – just compare two of Britain's best-known professional punters, Patrick Veitch and Harry Findlay – and Segal, Coton and Collier all brought their own personalities to the Pricewise column.

"It sounds a bit arty, but I've always said that people should bet according to how they see the world," Segal explains. "If you're a guy who hides behind the sofa when you've had 50 quid on a horse, then just have a fiver. If you're a laid-back character who doesn't mind long losing runs then back big-priced horses. If you need regular winners, back a few short-priced ones. Get yourself in form. And remember, there are plenty of opportunities to back winners."

Jamie Spencer is one of Tom Segal's favourite jockeys in big handicaps

NEVER UNDERESTIMATE THE ROLE OF THE JOCKEY

Regular readers of Pricewise will know the jockeys who are held in the highest regard by Segal (chief among these household gods are Ruby Walsh over the jumps and Jamie Spencer on the flat). Segal is outraged by the perceived wisdom that the horse is the only thing that matters and that jockeys don't make a difference to the result.

"Try telling that to Tony McCoy!" he exclaims. "I'm sure if you said to McCoy that he was only as good as some bloke who rides one winner a year he'd be pretty pissed off! The jockeys are the only humans who can affect the race once it's started. Obviously, the ability of the horse is hugely important but it's the same as an athletics or a cycling race – if you go too fast too soon, or you get too far behind, or you're on the wrong part of the track, then you're not going to win, even if you're the best in the race.

"It's vital to make sure that you have confidence in the jockey before you back a horse. The number of times I've kicked myself for tipping one ridden by a jockey I don't rate is ridiculous. I knew I didn't like him but I thought the horse would get him out of trouble. Every punter knows that feeling, when you're sitting there thinking 'Jesus Christ, what a terrible ride – why did I back him?' So to deny that jockeys have an influence – a major influence – on a race is absolute nonsense."

Any conversation with Segal about jockeyship is bound to throw up the name of Ruby Walsh sooner rather than later. Walsh first shot to prominence – in England, at least – as a 20-year-old winning the Grand National on Papillon in April 2000. Trained by Ruby's father Ted, the horse was well backed after being selected by three *Racing Post* tipsters – Mel Cullinan, Mel Collier in Pricewise and Segal in the Spotlight verdict.

"I make no bones about it," Segal says. "Spotting Ruby Walsh all those years ago was one of the main things that got me where I am today. He is absolutely the best jockey I've ever seen over jumps and he's been great for me, just like Jamie Spencer has been on the flat. Some people still don't like Spencer but he and Richard Hughes are the best jockeys in the races that I tend to do, the big handicaps. It's all about patience. Most jockeys are so gung-ho – in these big handicaps they go so fast; they go bonkers, because there are 30 runners. Spencer has the confidence to ride the race the way it should be ridden, sitting and waiting.

"I know if I'm watching a Royal Ascot race on the straight track that there's no way Jamie Spencer is going to be in the lead at any stage before the final furlong. He'll be waiting and waiting and waiting. And in an Ascot handicap when they've gone off too fast and it's uphill, the more patient you can be as a jockey, the better. They'll all be coming back to you at the finish. Amazingly there are still people who bang on about Spencer or Hughes, saying 'he left that one too much to do' when invariably their horses will have got the best position they could – precisely because of the way they were ridden. If they'd been ridden differently they'd probably have finished last.

"It's the same with Ruby at Cheltenham. You see so many of his rides where he's sitting last and everyone's saying 'bloody hell, he's messed this up' and he comes and wins because the rest of them kill themselves up the hill. McCoy is a different type of jockey – very strong, better at forcing the issue – but Wayne Hutchinson is another who I think is tremendous over the jumps.

"Of course, in a seven-runner race at Windsor when they go really slow, you wouldn't want to be sitting last like Spencer does. It didn't quite work for him at Ballydoyle, perhaps because he was riding those Group horses as though he was riding handicappers. But he's stuck to what he does best in those big handicaps and it works. You'd be staggered at how many of those kind of races he and Richard Hughes win.

"You have to remember that I'm different from most tipsters and punters in that I only really deal with the big races. That's my area of expertise. Don't ask me about a race at Fontwell, because I wouldn't have the first clue what it takes to win there. Maybe in races like that the jockeys don't have any impact at all but those aren't the races I'm asked to tip on. I can only do what I'm asked to do and in my opinion the most crucial aspect of any big race is the jockey."

GET TO KNOW YOUR TRAINERS

It isn't necessary to join the dawn chorus on the Newmarket gallops to develop a profitable relationship with the top trainers. By reading quotes in the *Racing Post*, monitoring trainers' websites and paying attention to interviews on Racing UK or At The Races, it's possible to get a sense of their plans and ambitions for certain horses.

"You can build up a feeling about a horse just from reading its trainer's quotes on the *Racing Post* database," Segal says. "If you do it for long enough, and read between the lines a bit, you'll get an insight into a trainer's personality. You start to see how he feels about a certain horse, whether he's positive or negative, and what his plans for it are likely to be. Sometimes a trainer will be talking about a maiden, a horse that's never won a race, and he'll say 'the long-term plan is Royal Ascot' or 'the long-term plan is the St Leger.' Immediately, then, you know he thinks the horse is pretty good. So you can keep an eye out for it and one day you might find it well handicapped, as it's progressing towards running in a good race.

"Of course, it might not live up to the stable's expectations but at least you know that the trainer has seen some inherent ability there. They see them day in, day out, remember, so you've got to trust them. I know some people don't like listening to trainers but if Henry Cecil, after 40 or 50 years in the game, can't tell a good horse from a bad one then something's wrong, isn't it? He clearly can."

Segal's job revolves around the big meetings and he admires the trainers who get their horses to peak at exactly the right time: "I like trainers who have targets for their horses. I much prefer the trainers who have a specific plan to those who are just shit-throwing, just seeing what happens as the season goes on. In other sports there's always talk about peaking – for the Olympics, for a title fight – and I like trainers who use their intelligence to get a horse to its best on a certain day."

Mark Coton is also keen on these kind of trainers – particularly his "all-time favourite" Major Dick Hern. Coton wrote in his 1990 book *Value Betting* that "the Major is a creature of habit. He likes to win the same races year in year out. Top of his list of targets are the Derby (three wins) and the St Leger (six), but he also has a predilection for races at all the big meetings. Armed with this information, the stable follower can take great pleasure in plotting his own campaign for the best horses in the yard and have his confidence bolstered when the Major takes the same view."

"John Gosden, William Haggas, Michael Bell and James Fanshawe have always targeted certain horses for Royal Ascot," Segal says. "They build them up for the big race. It's the same with Jonjo O'Neill at Cheltenham. Now, I don't watch them train every day so I might end up on the wrong horse, on the one that doesn't peak on the right day, but invariably Jonjo or Gosden or Haggas will have horses that run really well at the big meetings. And I love following trainers like that.

"There's a lot of nonsense talked about trainers. If Gosden is running a horse in a Royal Ascot handicap that's only won a stupid maiden at Southwell or somewhere, people will say 'that one's got an awful lot to find on the form book.' Yes, it might have a lot to find on the form book but it also happens to be trained by John Gosden. He's got 150 horses, he's won this race countless times before and he knows exactly the level of horse that he needs to win it again. So for Gosden to be running it is a tip in itself. You might get 10-1 about a horse when it should really be a 5-1 shot. Now, purely on the formbook, it's a 20-1 shot but I'm always prepared to believe that the trainer knows how good his horse is.

"From a tipping perspective, you need a bit of confidence to actually tip those sort of horses because if they finish last you'll get some flack. People will ask why you've tipped something at Royal Ascot that's only ever won a Southwell maiden. That's the hard bit, having confidence in your own ability and your own theory. Sometimes when I'm on a bad run, the temptation is to play it safe – go for the horse that's top on the ratings, because that's the obvious tip. But being able to find those tricky ones, the ones most people aren't looking at, is going to pay off in the long run.

"As tipsters and racing writers, we say what we think about a horse and 99 per cent of the time the trainer will know whether or not we're talking crap. Now and again he might be surprised by a horse's performance – we might be right and he might be wrong – but he's the one on the inside. He knows how the preparation has gone, how the horse is eating, if he's had any injuries – all these things, which we don't generally know, are in the trainer's possession. You have to have faith in the top trainers so if there's a Gosden horse running in an Ascot handicap with no great credentials, it'll be the first one on my shortlist. Because for it to be targeted at Ascot, the chances are that it's an awful lot better than it's shown so far."

REMEMBER THE HUMAN FACTOR

Hopefully the previous two sections have exploded the old punters' myth that jockeys and trainers are the worst judges in racing. Studying a trainer's habits and working patterns can be instructive and, if you look hard enough, there are clues and signposts everywhere. The significance of jockey bookings is well known but Segal also recommends close scrutiny of where each trainer sends their most promising two-year-olds or novices.

"I always think that's quite interesting," he says. "Most trainers have a profile of how their best horses have got to the top in the past and they tend to stick to the same route. I spoke to Philip Hobbs about this recently and he said that he usually sends his best novice chasers to Exeter. William Haggas regularly runs his best maidens at Newbury. It's always useful to see where people are willing to start a horse that they think is above average. Trainers have this profile of what best suits their horses – they know which track, which day, which ground has worked well for them before – and that's where they'll run them. It's all part of the progression towards a big race.

"Aidan O'Brien had never really used the 2,000 Guineas as a trial for the Derby until this year with Camelot. In the past all his main Derby contenders have run over in Ireland, in the Leopardstown Derby trial. This year, though, he did it a different way – he used the Guineas as a prep race for the Derby for Camelot. I like keeping an eye on those trends and trying to work out what a trainer might be thinking before it comes to the big race."

The human factor doesn't end with the trainer, however. Segal suggests that taking note of a horse's connections can also pay off now and again. "There was a Willie Mullins horse which won a big hurdle a few years back and one of my reasons for tipping it was that the owner was sponsoring the race. Mullins said afterwards that they'd been planning to win this race for a long time. Luckily I'd remembered hearing him say a couple of years earlier – maybe at a Cheltenham preview or on the telly – that this hurdle race was the horse's long-term target.

"I wouldn't suggest following that sort of thing blind – if Marwan Koukash is sponsoring a race at Chester then he's going to have a runner in it anyway so it doesn't tell you much. If you use your brain, though, it can throw up a few winners. You can Google anything these days so if you do a bit of research, you never know what you might find out."

Segal's attention to detail helped unearth a winner on the Saturday of Royal Ascot in 2012 when he opposed the hot favourite for the Chesham Stakes, Move To Strike, with the 7-1 shot Tha'ir. As his preview explained, the Godolphin colt "couldn't have been more impressive at Ripon last time out when seeming to surprise his connections. I always think that is a good sign in a horse."

"One of my strengths is probably prioritising the human element in racing," he says. "I concentrate on jockeys and trainers and stables because they have a much bigger effect on the outcome than many people think – and, of course, that's reflected in the market."

LEARN TO IDENTIFY PROBLEM HORSES

Segal is adamant that punters should look beyond the form book and the official ratings when analysing a horse's ability. He admits that his personal approach is "difficult to define. I always get in trouble when I'm discussing this sort of angle because there's no secret per se – I just look at the way horses move, the way they hold themselves. I'm interested in a horse's demeanour, the position of its head, the way it travels. Obviously, all this is in the eye of the beholder but that's what I'll be looking out for in a race.

"It's not an exact science. There are certain horses that I just couldn't have – I've never been a great Kauto Star fan although I was clearly wrong about him! It was just the way he came off the bridle when he was under pressure that made me think something was hurting him. And I think the worst attribute for a horse is pulling too hard. I don't like any horse that pulls hard. I'll sometimes tip them in the hope that they'll settle down but most of the time they run rubbish.

"Over the years I feel I've been pretty good at spotting horses that have problems. Immediately after Black Caviar ran at Ascot [in 2012] I said to my mate James Willoughby 'that horse is injured.' I could see that there was something wrong with the horse because it never galloped to the line, its head never went down. At no stage during the race did it look happy.

"Now most people might not have looked at the race in that way. My first port of call when I'm watching racing is the horse, just watching what it's doing and how it's doing it. I'm not looking at jockeys, I'm not looking at positions or tactics, I'm just looking at how a horse is going through the race. I'm not sure if that's peculiar to me or if it's something that other people could take on board but that's just the way that I watch a race."

Black Caviar, the Australian mare dubbed the Wonder from Down Under, maintained her unbeaten record in the Diamond Jubilee Stakes at Ascot – but only just. Jockey Luke Nolen blamed himself for the dramatic margin of victory – she beat Moonlight Cloud by a head – but Segal's attention was fixed on the horse. "For me, Black Caviar had something wrong with her. I wasn't necessarily keen to take her on at Ascot because I didn't know too much about her, or about the standard of Australian racing in general, so I presumed that everyone was right and that she was the fastest thing in the world. Because of all the fuss about the jockey, people would have made excuses for that Ascot performance and if she had run again in Britain she'd still probably have gone off at 1-7 or 1-8. But having seen the race with my own eyes, I would never have backed that horse again in a million years. Never."

SPOTTING POTENTIAL IS THE KEY

Segal's intuitive approach to racing means he revels in the educated guesswork that is required for ante-post betting. "I've lost count of the number of times I've seen horses that I thought were the second coming but have turned out to be nothing special," he confesses. "Obviously you're going to get it wrong a lot of the time but when you get it right it's fantastic. Sea The Stars is probably the one I've enjoyed most. Even when I saw him as a two-year-old, winning Mickey Mouse races in Ireland, I felt there was something brilliant about him, which proved to be the case.

"It's always nice to feel that you're the first person on the bandwagon. I've never been good at following – I find it hard to tip horses that everybody else is already on. It's like being a football reporter. If you spot a good player at Crewe and give him a great write-up in the paper and then he turns out to be the lad [Nick Powell] who's signed by Manchester United for £6m then it's a brilliant feeling. It's just the same for Steve Palmer [the *Racing Post*'s golf tipster]. He spotted that big Belgian lad, Nicolas Colsaerts, before anybody else and he's been winning ever since."

The manner in which Sea The Stars won his races – none of his eight victories were by a margin wider than two-and-a-half lengths – emphasised Segal's advice to watch races rather than rely on the bare form. "I might get word that a horse is very good," he says, "but I prefer to see it with my own eyes. Anyway, by the time I get the word about a horse, everybody else will have already backed it, so it's not going to be a viable Pricewise tip. I'm not looking at what a horse has already done; I'm looking for what it might do in the future. I'm looking for potential."

The *Racing Post*'s David Ashforth memorably defined the formbook as being "useful for predicting what will happen in the past" and Segal shares that view. "Most people work around the form of what a horse has done in the past," he points out. "They look at the Timeform ratings, the *Racing Post* ratings, whatever. But if punters and bookmakers are all looking at the same things, then it's no use to me. I'm not interested in all that pounds-for-lengths stuff. It's a horse race – the jockey can get stopped for a second, which is worth more than a pound. I can understand the old-fashioned form men writing about all that but if they could do it, the bookies could do it and everyone could do it. So the one with the highest Timeform rating is going to be up there near the head of the market.

That's all well and good, but it's not the angle I want to be coming from.

"I want to find the one that's got progression in it. I'd say 90 per cent of punters go on what a horse has already achieved on the racecourse, which seems ridiculous to me. They're suggesting that no horse is ever capable of improving, when probably 90 per cent of races are won by improvers. Almost every single race is won by a horse that has run better than it did last time out or the few times before that. So I'm not looking for the ones which are already top-rated – I'm looking for the ones that are going to be top-rated next time out.

"In jumps racing, it's no secret that I like Irish horses in handicap chases – the ones with great potential. I think jumps horses tend to get a bit sick of racing. It's very hard to maintain their enthusiasm. That's something Paul Nicholls does brilliantly– he manages to maintain his horses' enthusiasm for the game, which not many trainers can do. But in general, over the jumps, I'd just be looking for an unexposed, improving horse."

DON'T READ TOO MUCH INTO THE MINUTIAE

Pricewise has never relied on traditional areas of race analysis and Segal is quick to dismiss the impact of the draw on modern-day racing. "I'm not a draw man at all," he says. "Probably around Mel's time, the draw was vital but it's changed since then. The draw had become such an influential part of the market that clerks of the course and trainers and journalists would spend their lives talking about it – some of them still do, in fact. If you look at the quotes in the paper they'll still say 'my one's got a bad draw' or 'this is well drawn' and most of the time it doesn't make a damn bit of difference – the jockeys all go down the middle and the best horse wins.

"So I actually like horses that are perceived to be badly drawn. They provide inherently better value than horses that are perceived to be drawn well. At Royal Ascot [in 2012] everybody was talking about what was a good draw but nobody really had a clue. I'm sure the draw made a difference in every race but I don't think anybody knows what a good or a bad draw is anymore so there's no point trying to bet around it.

"The other thing people often worry about too much is the distance. In my opinion, the trip is the most overrated thing in racing. Henry Cecil said that he couldn't run Frankel over seven furlongs because it would be like Usain Bolt running a marathon. It's not like that at all. The best horses are the best horses. If you're a fast horse, you're going to be a fast horse over five or six furlongs. Five furlongs is still quite a long way – it's a pretty good distance, a kilometre or so. Obviously if a horse doesn't stay a trip, then that's different. There are horses who can't produce their best over a longer trip but then it's all about the opposition. Steve Ovett used to win 5000m races and 1500m races. If you're a fast horse, you're a fast horse."

Segal's confidence in Frankel's versatility was supported by a couple of top jockeys. Richard Hughes wrote in the *Racing Post*: "Quite frankly, whatever Frankel runs in, Frankel will win. We are in the era of a unique horse who, if connections let him, could win the July Cup and the Arc in the same season." And Hayley Turner agreed, claiming in her column on the Monday after Royal Ascot that "he has the speed for the July Cup and the stamina for the Prix de l'Arc de Triomphe."

While Segal is keen on trainers' quotes, he advises punters not to read too much into racing punditry in general. "Talking about the minutiae – the draw, the trip, the going – is what keeps racing ticking over. People in racing probably have 20,000 races to talk about every year and a lot of it is very boring. They have to find something to say on telly so they talk about 'soft-ground horses' or runners 'dropping back in trip' but they don't really know the horse. The problem is that there's not much else to say about these kind of horses because they're very moderate.

"One example is when a horse is described as being 'unlucky' last time out. It will almost certainly be overbet for its next race because they'll show the replay and point out how it 'should' have won. But many horses are unlucky and many horses are lucky. It's just that, with two racing channels and the *Racing Post* coming out every day, not much gets through the net these days."

Analysing the minutiae of racing certainly used to be a profitable punting strategy. As more and more information becomes freely available to mainstream punters, however, tipsters such as Segal need to explore new avenues: "I think when I started doing Pricewise it was much easier than it is now. The whole thing has moved on a long way, in my opinion and, as I said, not much gets through the net nowadays."

BE WARY ABOUT BETTING ON FLAT RACING WHEN THE GROUND IS SOFT

Segal has had more cause than most to bemoan the rain-lashed summer of 2012. "I had a terrible run on the flat at the start of the season," he admits. "Obviously I tipped some bad horses but I'd say it's mainly down to the ground. When there is this much rain you simply don't know what the ground is. People say 'it's soft' but soft ground at Chester is totally different from soft ground at Newmarket or Ascot.

"I'd actually recommend not betting on flat racing when it's soft, if you can help it. Horses aren't trained to be raced on soft ground so it's total guesswork whether or not a horse will go on the ground. And there is such a variety of goings under the label 'soft ground' – a horse can go on soft ground at Newmarket, for example, and then hate it at Chester.

"I always do miles better on the flat when the ground is good, good to firm. On fast ground, it's just about the best horse. It's about quantifying ability and potential whereas on soft ground it's much more about who handles the conditions, which you can't usually predict with any great confidence. A horse might have won on heavy ground in the past but the heavy ground it won on will have been totally different from the heavy ground it's running on now.

"There was a race at York the other day where a horse won by 15 lengths – it could have won by 115 – because it was the only one who went on the ground. But it had never run on soft ground before so nobody had any idea that it would handle it so well. Of course, you can still find winners when it's soft but there's no point making it sound as though you're confident about your tips. It does come down to guesswork, I'm afraid."

Shortly after this interview was conducted, Segal emerged from the quagmire of the flat season with a pair of winners on Northumberland Plate day at Newcastle. There was no feigned confidence behind his tips, however, and his column began: "Flat-bred horses are not supposed to race on heavy ground so it's anyone's guess who will handle conditions at Newcastle and The Curragh today." Segal predicted the Northumberland Plate would come down to "survival of the fittest" and added that "I wouldn't be surprised if there were a couple of furlongs between first and last." Some educated guesswork pointed Pricewise followers in the direction of a 6-1 shot for the Northumberland Plate. "One horse we know will relish the test is Chester Cup winner Ile De Re, who galloped on strongly through the heavy ground to beat Overturn and is arguably the only horse in the race who will be ideally suited by conditions." Donald McCain's stayer ticked another key box for Segal, as "he has been trained for this race, too."

Earlier in the card, Maarek – "incredibly impressive on soft ground at Newmarket under a big weight at the start of the season [...] plenty of form in heavy ground in Ireland" – won the Group 3 sprint, having been advised at 9-2. That double may have had Pricewise punters singing in the rain but it failed to convert Segal to the joys of soft-ground betting. In his column the next day he wrote that his 'punting high' of the week was "a couple of winners on heavy ground at Newcastle. Wonders will never cease."

DON'T BE INTIMIDATED BY BIG-FIELD RACES

It is no coincidence that so many of Pricewise's finest moments have come in big-field sprint handicaps. The likes of Santo Padre (tipped at 22-1 for the Portland Handicap at Doncaster in 2009), Evens And Odds (a 33-1 winner of the Stewards Cup at Goodwood in 2010) and Dandy Boy (advised at 25-1 when winning Ascot's Victoria Cup, also in 2010) reflect Segal's enjoyment of such races.

"It's hard to pick out the winners that have given me most satisfaction," he says. "They're not always the obvious ones. People always talk about Grand National and Gold Cup winners but there are loads of sprint handicappers over the years which have been really satisfying. Those sort of handicaps seem to suit my temperament – probably because I like to be the clever arse! Anyone can find the winner of the Derby – there's usually only two or three horses you'd say can win it – but to find the winner of a 20-runner sprint handicap or a big handicap hurdle is something else.

"Again, it depends on what kind of punter you are. If you're going to worry about having ten straight losers then don't bet in big-field handicaps because you'll have those sort of barren runs all the time. If you want to back 6-4 shots every week and say you're a brilliant punter, that's all well and good. I think consistently finding short-priced winners is hard, myself, especially in racing. If you want to back 6-4 shots, why not do it in football? At least when you back a football team at those odds, you know the players, you know the opposition and the context of the game. That has to be better than taking a short price about an animal when you have no idea, really, about how its preparation for the race has gone or how it's feeling on the day.

"I think handicaps provide great value for punters, though. Don't be put off by a big field – you can quickly narrow it down to five or six runners. If you're any good – and you'll soon work out whether you're any good or not – you can narrow it down to five or six, then back a couple of those at 10-1 or bigger. That's how I approach these big handicaps. When I look at them, there are all these horses at massive prices that I could easily make a case for, whether it's because of trainer form or a jockey booking or just the way I feel they're going to run.

"And that's why Betfair works. That's why there are big drifters and big movers on the flat, because people find out that the original prices were totally wrong. People don't want to back a horse at 14-1 on the morning of a race but, five minutes before the off, they can't get enough money on the same horse at 6-1. They've found out extra details about the horse or about the race and those details mean that the 6-1 is really good value, even though they've missed the early 14-1."

Pricewise's fine record in big-field handicaps has contributed to a change in the way punters regard these races. In September 2009, Segal picked the winner of the Ayr Bronze Cup – 33-1 shot Baldemar – and followed up the next day by tipping Kaldoun Kingdom, who was backed from 16-1 in to 8-1 when landing the Ayr Silver Cup. Victor Chandler spokesman Neal Wilkins told the *Racing Post* afterwards that "the great thing with Mr Segal is that he makes some of his shrewdest selections in races that people used to think of as bookies' benefits, but that are now rapidly becoming nightmares for the layers."

"I can totally understand people who don't like betting in those kind of races, though," Segal says. "Mark Coton was never a big handicap punter, for instance, but it just happens to suit my style of tipping and my approach to racing."

Asked for a summary of his approach to punting, Segal returns to his only golden rule: "Keep it fun, that's the key to any gambling. Don't let it mean too much. If it means too much then it hurts when you lose and if it hurts when you lose, that's a problem. Just try to keep it nice and calm and fun."

A WEEK IN THE LIFE
OF TOM SEGAL

Tony McCoy and Tom Segal share the front-page spotlight after Synchronised triumphs in the 2012 Cheltenham Gold Cup.

PRICEWISE TARGETS the biggest races and the most competitive betting heats which is why the column's followers have enjoyed so many glorious winners at the Cheltenham Festival and Royal Ascot. Those winners don't come easily, however. While British and Irish racing fans experience Cheltenham from the comfort of their armchairs or the murky recesses of the Guinness Village, the Festival is a frantic affair for Tom Segal.

In this chapter, Segal reveals his daily routine for Cheltenham 2012, from the boozy preview evenings and optimistic ante-post tips to the moment on Friday evening when he can, at last, put his feet up – or start preparing for next year's extravaganza.

SUNDAY, MARCH 11

The Cheltenham Festival casts a long shadow over the National Hunt season and Segal believes that punters should avoid making up their minds about particular horses or specific races too early in the winter.

"The problem a lot of people have is that they do their thinking about Cheltenham before they actually know who's running and what the conditions are," he says. "I tend to avoid thinking about Cheltenham until as late as possible. Obviously that's not always possible when you're doing Pricewise because of the *Racing Post*'s ante-post feature. That starts in January so I'll be tipping on one race per week in the paper for the ten weeks leading up to Cheltenham.

"From the start of January I'll be looking at the individual races and trying to pick out horses with the right profiles – the type of horse that might win at Cheltenham. This year my ante-post tipping was rubbish but in the past I've done pretty well with it."

One ante-post highlight for Segal's followers was the Wednesday of the 2006 Festival when Newmill won the Queen Mother Champion Chase and Star De Mohaison took the Royal & SunAlliance Chase. Both had been tipped by Pricewise at 33-1 in the build-up to Cheltenham and Segal maintains that the ante-post markets can offer excellent value. "In this day and age, ante-post betting is really good," he says. "Because of the introduction of Betfair, the markets are incredibly accurate come the day of the race. They're at their most accurate five minutes before the race but punters still have the chance to back big-priced winners if they're betting the day or the week before the race.

"Of course, every year there are loads of ante-post tips that, come the day of the race, I wish I could chuck out. You have to remember that I'm tipping ten weeks in advance sometimes so a horse has probably had one or two runs since then. And the bookmakers are betting on next year's races the day after Cheltenham finishes so the markets are quite mature even by the time I start doing my ante-post tips in January. I'm looking for an angle in but it's not always obvious. I'd say 60 or 70 per cent of the ante-post stuff I wouldn't tip again if I had the opportunity. But then there are the 30 per cent where you might think 'that's a good bet, that's a really good bet.' And they tend to be at big prices so if you're coming into a race having backed a 20-1 shot that's now trading at 6-1, it's clearly a great bet.

"For the most part, I leave it as late as possible to look at the individual races. I go to Ireland and do a few Cheltenham preview nights. I find those quite helpful because they let you see under the skin. You hear what the trainers really think about their horses rather than everybody just saying 'this is a good horse.' You get to know the ins and outs, what the horses have been doing, whether they've been working well, which is what I like to find out about. That's how I've always worked, thinking about how horses have been prepared and how they're likely to come into a race. So speaking to the trainers or jockeys can help – it can put you off a horse or make you feel more confident about one that you're tipping.

"But these previews are mainly just fun nights. A whole lot of shit is talked – most notably by me – and we're mostly talking about the major races. People want to hear about Hurricane Fly and Kauto Star, horses like that, so it's unlikely to sway my opinion about horses that I know so well. It's only when I get to talk to a couple of trainers on a one-to-one basis afterwards that I'll ask about their runner in a certain handicap or whatever and that can be helpful."

The Sunday before Cheltenham is the calm before the storm for Segal. His ante-post portfolio is bulging – hopefully with a healthy percentage of "great bets" – but he must wait until the fields are confirmed before setting about Tuesday's races.

"We know all about the big races – on the first day it's the Champion Hurdle and we might have the 48-hour declarations so we know who's going to run in that. But I'm not too interested in the big races because they're mature markets by this stage and I've already tipped on them ante-post. When it comes to the Cheltenham week Pricewise, I'm looking at the races that nobody has looked at before. There's no point studying up on the handicaps before the runners are confirmed because you'll spend half the time looking at horses that you don't need to look at. So I'd wait until the day before to look at those races."

MONDAY, MARCH 12

Segal's working week begins at around 11am as he starts to research and write his Pricewise previews for Tuesday's *Racing Post*. "I'll have been thinking about Cheltenham, obviously," he says. "I'll have a fair idea of what's likely to run because the advance declarations give me an overview of each race. I'll know which trainers' horses are running well, which jockeys have dropped out and what the ground is going to be. And I'll have spoken to the bookies to find out their each-way terms so by the day before the race I'll be purely looking at the runners themselves."

Segal's interest in Irish racing is an integral part of his Cheltenham preparation: "It always amazes me that you still hear people on television saying 'I don't know about that one, I don't follow the Irish form.' Well, it's on the telly, it's in the paper – it's not a state secret. How people will happily watch a race from Cartmel but won't watch one at Punchestown is beyond me. It's like being given the choice between watching a League Two match or watching Barcelona.

"Ireland has the best trainers in the world. On the flat, Aidan O'Brien has the strongest stable in the world by miles and Jim Bolger and John Oxx are another two of the world's best trainers. Over jumps they've got Willie Mullins, who is a sensational trainer; they've got the best jockeys – Ruby Walsh and Barry Geraghty and Tony McCoy, who goes over there a lot; and they've got horses like Hurricane Fly.

"It's just better racing, full stop. Because the Irish system is set up with only a few meetings a week, the quality of the average race is miles better than in England. If you go to a maiden at Fairyhouse, Aidan O'Brien will probably have a runner; go to a maiden at Bath and you're struggling to recognise any of the trainers' names.

"Watching Irish racing has definitely helped me find winners. It's been one of my favourite angles. I haven't got that advantage anymore because others have caught on to it but for many years English people didn't appreciate the worth of the Irish form.

"I went to an Irish point-to-point a few weeks before Cheltenham and all the top trainers were there. The winner of a point-to-point was bought for £200,000. They just love their racing. I spoke to Ted Walsh about it once and he told me that the difference between Ireland and England is that in England kids want to be David Beckham or Wayne Rooney; in Ireland they want to be Ruby Walsh. Racing is woven into the fabric of their society. It's in their nature.

"From a tipping and punting perspective the great thing about Ireland is that lots of people have horses there. Obviously, people have worked out that Aidan O'Brien is going to win every Classic going, pretty much, and that Willie Mullins is a great trainer but the farmer down the road will also have a horse – and it might be a very good horse. Every year at Cheltenham there will be plenty of good horses and good trainers from Ireland that nobody in England is talking about."

TUESDAY, MARCH 13

Race	Horse Stake	SP	Result		
1.30	*Midnight Game*	*1pt at 14-1*	18-1	*15th/19*
1.30	*Vulcanite*	*1pt at 20-1*	22-1	*10th/19*
2.00	*Menorah*	*1pt at 16-1*	10-1	*3rd/6*
2.40	The Package	1pt at 7-1	6-1	4th/19
2.40	**Alfie Sherrin**	**1pt at 25-1**	**14-1**	**WON**
3.20	Oscars Well	1pt e-w at 25-1	14-1	6th/10
4.00	Dancing Tornado	1pt at 25-1	11-1	Unseated rider
4.40	Shop DJ	1pt e-w at 20-1	10-1	5th/19

Ante-post selections in italic; winners in bold

"At every Cheltenham Festival there are horses who are talked up as good things," Tuesday's Pricewise column began. "And, like Cue Card and Dunguib over the past two years, they often get beaten. I can't see the same happening this year because today's curtain-raiser sees three horses likely to start odds-on in Sprinter Sacre, Hurricane Fly and Quevega and all look bombproof."

Such outstanding favourites pose problems for Pricewise. Sprinter Sacre and Hurricane Fly were no bigger than even-money in the morning while Coral's 8-13 was the top price about Quevega. That 8-13 may have represented great value in hindsight – Willie Mullins's mare won comfortably at an SP of 4-7 – but Segal hasn't made his name by tipping 8-13 shots.

"It was a funny first day this year," he says. "Quevega is always in a terribly weak race so there's nothing to beat her. Sprinter Sacre just looked like something I'd never seen before. But when I did the ante-post tip on the Arkle I couldn't give Sprinter Sacre at 7-4 six weeks before the race – that's not really what Pricewise is about. I tipped Menorah, who finished third, ante-post and there were only six runners on the day so I couldn't have another tip. I thought Sprinter Sacre was going to win and I didn't want to tip two horses in a six-runner race, particularly against a favourite who I thought was bombproof. Normally I'd love to have a tip in the Arkle but this year it just wasn't a Pricewise type of race.

"It was a similar story in the Champion Hurdle. I already had Oscars Well running for me at 25-1 ante-post and I reckoned that Hurricane Fly couldn't be beaten. I obviously got that wrong [the 4-6 favourite finished third behind Rock On Ruby and Overturn] although I think subsequent events proved he should have won, really."

Having put a line through the races involving Sprinter Sacre, Hurricane Fly and Quevega, Segal focused his attention on the JLT Specialty Handicap Chase – a "tricky" contest, as he warned readers. Heeding his own advice about being flexible and open-minded, he wrote that "all week I've been keen on Quantitativeeasing, but it won't be easy for him off top weight." He deserted Nicky Henderson's runner, who went off an 11-2 joint-favourite but could finish only seventh, in favour of David Pipe's The Package and 25-1 shot Alfie Sherrin, who was trained – crucially – by Jonjo O'Neill.

"I went for Alfie Sherrin simply because I'm a massive fan of Jonjo O'Neill at the big meetings," Segal explains. "I'd kept my eye on Alfie because, although he'd shown nothing for years, he'd been very expensive. I think JP McManus had bought him out of Paul Nicholls' yard for a lot of cash. I'd seen him run in a handicap hurdle at Haydock in February and he finished his race off really well. I don't normally like those fast-finishers – they're often overbet the next time they run – but on this occasion Alfie Sherrin was still 25-1 in the morning, he looked as though he was running back into form and he had a really good chance.

"Jonjo has a great record in these handicap chases at Cheltenham. He seems to do it every year. He'd won it two years earlier with Wichita Lineman and I just felt that I couldn't ignore a horse of Jonjo's who was a 25-1 shot and had shown last time out that he was coming back to form."

The Pricewise verdict on Alfie Sherrin in Tuesday's paper concluded: "He's still relatively unexposed and if he can jump properly he has the ability to win races like this off his current mark." So it proved, as jockey Richie McLernon drove Alfie Sherrin on in the final furlong to hold off Fruity O'Rooney by a length, with The Package back in fourth.

"The Package had been off for a bit and he ran a really nice race too," Segal recalls. "It was my type of race, a big-field handicap, and it had a nice shape to it. It was just the kind of race that I like doing – there were a few at the top of the market that I didn't fancy, like Hold On Julio and Our Mick so it had a nice betting shape to it as well."

Alfie Sherrin's win vindicates another piece of Segal's punting wisdom – don't be afraid to back two horses in the same race. "If people are betting on the World Cup or the Masters golf, they'll have a few different bets, won't they?" he argues. "Why should a horse race be any different? There are 20 runners, there are 20 fences – it's not that easy to find the winner. Have a couple of cracks. In a really big field, I'd happily back three or four but I don't think that's fair on the readers. If they saw that I'd picked three in a race, they'd be thinking 'which one am I supposed to back?' But I always think it's a good idea to have a couple of horses running for you in those big handicaps."

WEDNESDAY, MARCH 14

Race	Horse	Stake	SP	Result	
1.30	Soll	1pt at 8-1	8-1	Brought down	
2.05	Batonnier	1pt at 12-1	-	Non-runner	
2.40	First Lieutenant	1pt at 16-1	9-2	2nd/9	
3.20	Wishful Thinking	1pt at 20-1	16-1	Fell	
4.00	Get Me Out Of Here	1pt at 10-1	6-1	2nd/28	
4.00	Silverhand	1pt at 25-1	25-1	4th/28	
4.40	Gorgeous Sixty	1pt at 14-1	8-1	19th/24	

A 25-1 winner on day one of the Festival eases the pressure on Segal but he is not inclined to get carried away. "It's the Cheltenham Festival," he says. "It's really hard. If this game was easy, everyone would be backing winners left, right and centre. Over the years I've managed to land a few winners but I'm certainly no genius. It's just down to a bit of luck, a bit of educated guesswork and getting to know what is required to win races at Cheltenham.

"I think some people find it hard to understand the factors that are really important in big races. Everyone can judge a horse's ability through its form or ratings but that isn't enough. It has to be able to run to that ability and I think I've generally been good at spotting which horses are going to put in a good performance at the right time."

The pressures of Pricewise mean that there is little time to savour Alfie Sherrin's victory. Segal's focus has already shifted to the following day's racing. "I don't get much time to enjoy Cheltenham as a racing fan," he admits. "While the racing is going on I'm working on the next day's column. I do all the price tables myself and during Cheltenham the bookies are changing their prices all the time so I'm constantly on the phone to them. I speak to the bookies and get the price tables into shape. Then I've got to write 2,000 words of copy for the next day's paper. The racing is on in the background and I'll watch all the races but I don't have time to be distracted by it."

One key factor that Segal monitors closely in the first couple of days of the Festival is trainer form. "Cheltenham is the be-all and end-all of the jumps season so I'm on the lookout for horses who have been trained for a particular race – trained for the minute really – and are in good form. It's not just the stable stars, either. I always think it's a good sign if a horse has run well at a big price, when nobody expected it to run well. That shows that the trainer has his horses in good shape. And that's what happened with Jonjo O'Neill and Alfie Sherrin. After he won on the Tuesday, I tipped quite a few Jonjo horses later in the week – Get Me Out Of Here, Sunnyhillboy, Synchronised – and they all ran really well.

"They wouldn't necessarily have been on my mind at the start of the week, especially not Sunnyhillboy, but I tipped him because Jonjo's horses had been running consistently well in similar kinds of races. That sort of staying, chasing-type horse tends to do well for Jonjo in the big festivals."

Wednesday's obvious Pricewise-type race is the Coral Cup, a 28-runner handicap in which Segal picked out the well-backed runner-up Get Me Out Of Here and 25-1 shot Silverhand, who ran a blinder to finish fourth. The near miss is an occupational hazard when tipping in such competitive races. "When you're having a bad run you half-expect everything to finish second, and they do, funnily enough," says Segal. "But when you're on a good run things seem to go right. You never notice the luck – you never notice the horse that was badly hampered and would have probably won if it had got a clear run.

"Alfie Sherrin had taken the pressure off slightly. If he hadn't won, then the Coral Cup would have been more frustrating, especially because the winner, Son Of Flicka, was very gettable. It hadn't shown anything for years but it was a very big price – 66-1 in the morning – and was well backed on the day. I felt it was the type of horse I could have found so to have the second and the fourth was annoying but they both ran well. There were 28 runners in the race and I found two that finished in the top four. If it was a golf tournament everyone would have said I was a genius!

"I was more frustrated with the last tip of the day, Gorgeous Sixty in the Fred Winter [a race Segal described in copy as "a nightmare on paper"]. That was a bad tip. I was never really happy with it. It hadn't shown enough and it didn't jump well enough. I knew that before the race but, given that it was a Willie Mullins horse with Ruby Walsh riding it, I expected things to come right on the day. I'm never very good when I'm expecting things to happen, though. I'm much better when I know what's going to happen.

"Sometimes I've got to give tips that I'm not confident or happy about. It's just part of the job – I've got a page to get out by 5pm and 800 words to write before deadline. But those are the annoying tips. They're the ones that get you down, the ones where you feel you've made a mistake. In hindsight, though, I would never have had the winner, Une Artiste. As long as I feel I've given a good tip – which I did with the two that were placed in the Coral Cup – then I can sleep well."

THURSDAY, MARCH 15

Race	Horse	Stake	SP	Result
2.05	Sergeant Guib's	1pt at 11-1	8-1	16th/24
2.05	Pineau De Roi	1pt at 33-1	16-1	14th/24
2.40	*Medermit*	*1pt at 9-1*	*8-1*	*3rd/12*
3.20	Thousand Stars	1pt at 12-1	8-1	4th/11
3.20	*Carlito Brigante*	*1pt e-w at 50-1*	*-*	*Non-runner*
4.00	Hectors Choice	1pt at 16-1	10-1	17th/22
4.40	**Sunnyhillboy**	**1pt at 8-1**	**13-2**	**WON**

Segal's approach to finding winners is intuitive – he relies on his feel for a race rather than exhaustive study of the formbook. It's an approach that has served him well at Cheltenham, where the size of the fields makes it almost impossible to analyse every horse in a race.

"It's slightly more difficult because there are so many runners and so much going on," he says. "I don't have quite as much time as I would in a normal day but that can work in my favour. Sometimes there's an 'analysis to paralysis' effect if I've only got one race to do. You can sit down and study that race for three or four hours but you end up going round in circles. You find reasons not to tip horses that you fancy, and that's a bad way to go about it. And you'd drive yourself mad if you tried to watch the video form for every single runner at Cheltenham."

Time is the major pressure during Cheltenham week. Pricewise is expanded to four pages of the *Racing Post* for each day of the Festival and the logistics of the operation leave Segal with little time for quiet contemplation. "This is the one thing that people always get wrong about Pricewise," he explains. "I probably have the least time of anyone in the whole world to actually look at the races. I'm not moaning – it's my job, obviously – but I have to get my copy over by 4pm or 5pm. The decs come out at 11am so I've literally got five hours, and three of those will be spent on the phone to bookies.

"I do the price tables myself, which I don't think Mel or Mark ever did. I like doing them, though. It keeps my rhythm going and it can be helpful to speak to the bookies. I like hearing what they've got to say, just the little tidbits. It's good to find out who's backed what – I don't take too much notice of it but it gives an indication of which way the market might go. So when it comes down to it, I have two hours to come up with the tips and write the column for the next day at Cheltenham. It's nothing like people expect it to be. Everyone else at the Festival probably spends five times longer looking at the races than I do."

Mel Collier spoke of the importance of the headline tip in building Pricewise's reputation and Thursday delivered a perfect example. "Sunnyhillboy an 8-1 cracker to bring joy to proceedings" ran the headline and the preview copy was equally bullish about the favourite's chances in the Fulke Walwyn Kim Muir Challenge Cup. "This is surely the day that Sunnyhillboy wins a big one," Segal wrote. "He remains a well-handicapped horse and comes from a stable whose horses have been running out of their skins this week. Jonjo O'Neill has no doubt targeted this race for Sunnyhillboy for a long time and he caught my eye at Haydock over hurdles last time in the same race Alfie Sherrin ran well in. We all know how well that horse performed on Tuesday."

Backed in to 13-2 by the off, Sunnyhillboy didn't disappoint. The *Racing*

Post's in-running comments concluded that he "led soon after last" and "forged clear" to win by four-and-a-half lengths. The tip also demonstrated that Pricewise isn't afraid to put up a good-value favourite, as Segal confirms: "6-4 shots can be great value if they're really 4-7 shots. Odds-on shots can be great value. Look at Frankel in the Queen Anne Stakes – he was 1-5 and he went off 1-10. People at the track obviously thought it was one of the best bets ever and it was – he won by half the track.

"Sunnyhillboy was a Jonjo O'Neill-inspired selection. That was the only reason for it, really. I knew the horse like the back of my hand, he'd run in so many big races, and this was probably the weakest race of the whole Festival. Jonjo had won the staying handicap chase on the first day, Sunnyhillboy had a good amateur jockey – all the pieces were there."

While O'Neill's fortunes went hand-in-hand with Pricewise at the 2012 Festival, Segal is keen to oppose some other trainers. "I think Paul Nicholls' horses at Cheltenham are always too short, especially his chasers," he says. "He's a nice bloke and he's very good with the press but everyone knows about his horses from day one – which ones he fancies, which ones the stable fancies – and it doesn't go unnoticed by the bookies. I always think his chasers are overhyped so they tend to go off at short prices and I want to take them on.

"Having said that, I've done very well with Paul Nicholls-trained horses over the years. I had Al Ferof ante-post at 25-1 for the Supreme Novices' in 2011 but the stable didn't fancy it – or they did fancy it, but it sprung up on them late on. That race is always won by a strong stayer. It's the first race of the Festival and they always go too fast. Al Ferof was held up out the back and came through to beat Sprinter Sacre. Now we know that Sprinter Sacre is a miles better horse but the way that first race is always run suits a massive stayer. That was the reason I tipped Al Ferof but Nicholls might not have seen it like that. He might have thought 'this is a stayer, he's probably not quick enough to win over two miles.' I'm not singling out Paul Nicholls but I think trainers in general don't always consider what each race entails. Of course, they know their horses better than anyone but they might not see what's needed to win a particular race."

FRIDAY, MARCH 16

Race	Horse	Stake	SP	Result	
1.30	Darroun	1pt at 16-1	14-1	13th/20	
1.30	Dodging Bullets	1pt at 25-1	20-1	4th/20	
2.05	Olafi	1pt at 14-1	13-2	16th/26	
3.20	**Synchronised**	**1pt at 14-1**	**8-1**	**WON**	
4.40	Toner D'Oudairies	1pt at 8-1	7-1	2nd/24	
4.40	Grandads Horse	1pt at 25-1	12-1	6th/24	
5.15	Slieveardagh	1pt at 14-1	9-1	11th/21	

Friday's Gold Cup was billed as a clash between defending champion Long Run and the people's choice Kauto Star. Typically, though, the iconoclastic Segal had a different view of the big race. "It was a good race to tip on from my perspective," he says. "Kauto Star was taking a big percentage out of the market and I had my doubts about him. I didn't think he was anywhere near as good at Cheltenham as he was at Kempton and bearing in mind his fall in the 2010 Gold Cup and the fact that he was a 12-year-old, I was prepared to take him on.

"Then there was Long Run, who'd been unimpressive at Newbury in his previous race. His trainer Nicky Henderson has a history of horses that don't go on and on so I thought he was beatable too. The market probably reflected what I was saying about people having very fixed ideas about Cheltenham. They know what they think about each race and they won't change their minds. They know that Kauto Star is very good and that Long Run is very good and because jumps horses are around for so long and the build-up to the Festival starts so early in the season, these opinions become set in stone. That's why I like betting at Cheltenham."

Identifying favourites that should be taken on is the first step; the next is picking the right horse with which to oppose them. Segal set the scene in his preview: "The Betfred Cheltenham Gold Cup has been all about Long Run and Kauto Star since the start of the season – nothing else has had a look-in. However, Cheltenham is never that simple and there are plenty more players than the betting would have you suggest. Burton Port comes into the reckoning after running Long Run close at Newbury and Midnight Chase is a Cheltenham specialist who looks sure to go well, but for me the horse that continues to be overlooked is Synchronised."

Synchronised's modest profile could hardly be blamed on Segal. Jonjo O'Neill's battler had been tipped by Pricewise for his wins in the Welsh National in January 2011 and the Lexus Chase at Leopardstown just after Christmas the same year. He had been backed from 20-1 in to 8-1 for the Lexus, a race in which he slammed fancied pair Rubi Light and Quito De La Roque. Segal, a not entirely unbiased observer, reckoned that Synchronised hadn't been given enough credit for his performance at Leopardstown.

"Synchronised was my favourite horse," he admits. "I'd tipped him to win the Welsh National and I'd tipped him to win the Lexus a couple of months before Cheltenham so I knew the horse back-to-front. He'd never won at Cheltenham before but I just had the impression that he was a better horse this year than he had been previously.

"People were still judging him on the days when he was running in handicap hurdles but he was clearly better than that. He'd run a really good race in a handicap hurdle to start with, then he'd won the Lexus by ten lengths. If Kauto Star had won the Lexus like that, or Long Run had, they'd have been 4-7 for the Gold Cup. But because it was Synchronised, he was still a 14-1 shot in the morning.

"Given how well Jonjo's horses had been going all week and given that the ground was testing – there was more rain forecast – I thought everything was right for him. And, as I said, it was a good race to have a bet in because the two favourites were opposable."

Segal made a strong case for the 14-1 headline selection. "I don't think I can remember a horse with his reserves of stamina," he wrote. "If Jonjo O'Neill's nine-year-old is close turning for home I don't think there is a horse in the field – and that includes Long Run – who will stay as well as him."

That bullish write-up saw Synchronised trimmed to 8-1 by the off but there was also an inevitable flood of money for Long Run (9-4 in to 7-4) and Kauto Star (3-1 from a best morning price of 9-2). Paul Nicholls' veteran was pulled up on the first circuit but at the business end of the race the indefatigable Synchronised, driven on by the equally indefatigable Tony McCoy, ground down the leaders late on, beating The Giant Bolster by just over two lengths with Long Run back in third.

While the Cheltenham crowd basked in the drama of the Gold Cup, Segal was soon brought back to earth. "I was really happy when Synchronised won – I felt I'd done a good job – but my tip a couple of races later was more important to me in a way. I put up Toner D'Oudairies to win the Martin Pipe Conditional Jockeys' Handicap and it was the most disappointing result of the year. It was only an 8-1 shot in a handicap but it should have won by 20 lengths. Everything went wrong for him and he was caught on the line by Attaglance but he really should have won by a long way. That's the nature of the job, though – ups and downs."

SATURDAY, MARCH 16

As another Cheltenham Festival comes to an end, the *Racing Post* asks its tipsters and reporters for the lessons they've learned from the week. Segal is reluctant to draw too many firm conclusions, however. "I find it quite difficult when I'm asked what I've learned from Cheltenham or Royal Ascot or whatever," he says. "Don't tip losers, I suppose! I'm sure there were lessons to be learned but I'll probably do the same things next year and every year after that. You tip the horses that you think are right at the time. Sometimes they're going to be the right ones and sometimes they'll be wrong.

"The paper asks me to pick a horse for a race at the following year's Festival. Last year I managed to fluke the winner of the Champion Chase, Finian's Rainbow, but I wouldn't really be thinking that far ahead. You can't take it too seriously. It's only horses running in a field. The point of betting and the point of racing has always been fun and enjoyment. Life is pretty boring in general these days. There's nothing to do apart from watch the telly so racing and punting is there to make life more bearable, more fun."

Segal had certainly helped make life more bearable for Pricewise followers during Cheltenham week. Ten of his 27 tips either won or were placed and his trio of Jonjo O'Neill-trained winners produced a profit of more than 20 points for the Festival.

PRICEWISE VERSUS THE BOOKIES

RACING POST Saturday 14 November 1987

● BETTING GUIDE ●

Robin looks the Bread winner at 10-1

EVENS..2-1..3-1..4-1..5-1..6-1..8-1..10-1..12-1..16-1..20-1

PRICEWISE

With The MORNING LINE

TRY a slice of 10-1 ROBIN WONDER in the Allinson Bread Handicap Hurdle (1.35) at Cheltenham today.

David Elsworth's gelding bids for his third win in this race and looks well worth an interest at the Ladbrokes odds.

Robin Wonder races off a 3lb lower mark than when doing the business convincingly here last term, and first time out is the time to catch him.

He also goes well on this course, a big advantage, and those with long memories will remember him running a marvellous second to See You Then in the 1985 Champion Hurdle. Last year's successful pilot Graham Bradley again takes the ride.

Careless

There are a number of dangers lurking at the bottom of the handicap, although the early betting tends to reflect this.

Celtic Shot did Pricewise readers proud at Sandown last time, beating Folk Dance impressively by 20 lengths, but has a stiffer task against today's opposition.

He is also still inclined to be careless at his hurdles and makes limited appeal at the morning 11-4, as does Heart Of Stone at 3-1, impressive though he was at Fontwell last time.

More interesting are Nos Na Gaoithe at the 13-2 offered by Mecca (Ladbrokes 9-2) and Cashew King at 8-1 with Ladbrokes (Corals 6-1).

A length and a half separated this pair at Wetherby last time and Cashew King, who gave the impression he needed the run then, is fancied to turn the tables on the soft ground.

Betting is taking a wide range on the **Mackeson Gold Cup (2.10)** with Very Promising (6-1) and Summons (6-1) edging out Tickite Boo (13-2 with Corals) and Beau Ranger (7-1) for favouritism.

Betting is likely to centre on this quartet, and readers of Wednesday's ante-post Pricewise will know this column's loyalties lie with

by MARK COTON

BEAU RANGER, although the morning 7-1 lacks the appeal of the 10-1 offered then.

Martin Pipe's nine-year-old is sure to run well off his favourable handicap mark and will like the soft ground, but Very Promising would prefer a sounder surface and has an extremely difficult task under 12st.

Summons and Tickite Boo are sure to command support and will probably start a point or so shorter than their morning prices, but both are only just out of the novice stage and seem to lack the experience usually needed for this tough handicap.

Pick of the other prices looks to be Malya Mal at the 11-1 offered by Mecca (Hills 8-1).

The Nicolet Instruments Handicap Hurdle (1.00) looks a tricky affair with a number of the runners unproven over the trip.

Difficult

TROY FAIR comes into this category, but those wanting an interest in this race are advised to take a chance on John Edwards' entire who looks fair value at the 10-1 offered by Chandlers, Coomes, Dennis and the Tote.

The five-year-old is a difficult ride, but is capable on his day, comes from a stable in fine form and enjoys a 5lb pull for four lengths with Ruby Flight on last month's Worcester form.

● Coomes and Dennis are betting early on the televised Wm A Swales Handicap Chase (1.30) at Newcastle and go 11-4 Comeragh King, Fergy Foster, 3 Raise An Argument, 11-2 Travelowen, 8 Barryphilips Disco, 10 Doronicum.

CHELTENHAM

1.00 Nicolet Instruments Handicap Hurdle
[10 DEC] Hcap 3m1f

HORSE	CHANDLER	COOMES	CORAL	DENNIS	W HILL	LADBROKES	MECCA	TOTE
MISS NERO	9-2	5	5	5	9-2	4	5	5
RUSTSTONE	6	6	5	6	6	5	5	11-2
MALFORD LAD	25	25	25	25	25	33	20	25
VON TRAPPE	11-2	6	6	6	7	8	13-2	6
EMO FOREVER	9-2	4	5	4	9-2	4	9-2	4
RUBY FLIGHT	13-2	7	6	7	6	7	6	13-2
TROY FAIR	10	10	8	10	9	9	9	10
MALADICTION	6	7	7	7	13-2	8	13-2	13-2
SAND CASTLE	11	10	12	10	10	11	12	12
TOUCH OF LUCK	16	16	16	16	14	14	16	16

Each-way 1/5 the odds a place 1,2,3.

1.35 Allinson Bread Hurdle (Handicap)
[9 DEC] (Listed Race) HcapL 2m

HORSE	CHANDLER	COOMES	CORAL	DENNIS	W HILL	LADBROKES	MECCA	TOTE
ROBIN WONDER	—	8	8	8	9	10	9	8
NOS NA GAOITHE	—	6	11-2	6	8	9-2	13-2	6
MUQADAR	—	16	14	16	14	16	14	14
SOLAR CLOUD	—	14	14	14	14	20	14	14
FIRM PRICE	—	6	7	6	13-2	6	13-2	6
HEART OF STONE	—	3	3	3	11-4	3	11-4	11-4
CASHEW KING	—	7	6	7	13-2	8	7	7
CELTIC SHOT	—	5-2	11-4	5-2	11-4	5-2	5-2	11-4
MY CHALLENGE	—	200	150	200	200	200	150	200

Each-way 1/5 the odds a place 1,2,3.

2.10 Mackeson Gold Cup Handicap Steeplechase (Listed Race)
[14 DEC] HcapL 2m4f

HORSE	CHANDLER	COOMES	CORAL	DENNIS	W HILL	LADBROKES	MECCA	TOTE
VERY PROMISING	6	6	5	6	6	6	6	6
SEA MERCHANT	14	16	16	16	16	18	16	16
WESTERN SUNSET	12	12	14	12	14	10	12	12
TICKITE BOO	6	6	13-2	6	11-2	6	6	6
VILLIERSTOWN	14	16	14	16	16	16	16	16
CAVVIES CLOWN	16	16	16	16	20	20	20	16
MALYA MAL	10	10	10	10	8	10	11	9
SUMMONS	11-2	6	11-2	6	11-2	6	11-2	6
BEAU RANGER	7	7	7	7	13-2	7	7	7
REPINGTON	14	14	14	14	16	12	16	16
FUDGE DELIGHT	10	8	8	8	10	10	10	10

By November 1987, Mark Coton's Pricewise column was accompanied by grids featuring bookmakers' early prices for the day's races.

PETER THOMAS'S 2007 profile of Mark Coton in the *Racing Post* began: "If you're planning to go into business as a poacher, then there's little doubt that the best place to learn the ropes is at gamekeepers' school." As discussed in Chapter One, Coton spent a largely unhappy spell working for Ladbrokes before he joined the *Racing Post* in 1986. It was an experience that laid the foundations for Pricewise because, as Thomas wrote, Coton's "time in the belly of the beast had whetted his appetite for bookies' blood."

Punters and bookmakers have always been uneasy bedfellows, grudgingly acknowledging their mutual dependence. A punter may have spotted the greatest bet of all time but it's worth nothing unless he can find a bookie who will lay it at the right price. A successful tipping service such as Pricewise, which feeds on early prices, brings another level of complexity and intrigue to the relationship between backers and layers.

John McCririck, an indomitable champion of punters' rights, believes that "Pricewise is a huge boon to punters and bookmakers hate it. They know that having the black-type prices in the *Racing Post* is very important for business but they also know those prices will come under pressure immediately if it's a Pricewise tip."

Channel 4's John McCririck was an influential early supporter of the Pricewise column

This chapter will examine the dilemma that faces bookmakers – namely that, as Oscar Wilde might have put it, the only thing worse than being in the Pricewise grids is not being in the Pricewise grids. Bookmakers' PR men and odds compilers share their memories of painful Pricewise-inspired gambles while Mark Coton, Mel Collier and Tom Segal talk about their run-ins with the bookies. The impact of the betting exchanges on the tipsters' craft will also be discussed, along with the age-old question of whether punters can get on Pricewise tips at the prices advertised in the *Racing Post*.

Coton had convinced his editor Graham Rock that the new column could work but he also required the cooperation of the bookmakers. A column called Pricewise that didn't have any prices would clearly have been a non-runner. "I had to persuade the bookies to do it over a period of weeks," Coton recalls. "I think my argument was that we weren't just talking about whether a horse was well handicapped or if its trainer was in form – we were bringing betting alive. If it works, I told the bookies, then it'll bring more people to your door. Initially they were all reluctant but then they thought 'well, if Coral are part of it, we'd better be part of it too.' And once John Thompson at Ladbrokes had said OK – he knew I had a lot of respect for him so he agreed to give me their early prices – everybody else thought 'if he's doing it, it must be alright.'

"But it wasn't straightforward, because the whole idea was hugely experimental. The *Racing Post* was also trying to get the bookmakers to advertise with us at the time but *The Sporting Life* carried a lot of weight in those days. I worried that the *Life* would block it, that they'd tell the bookies advertising with them that they couldn't give me their early prices.

"The bookmakers certainly took a bit of persuading but I used to say to them 'look, you're sending press releases to our news desk saying that this has been backed or that's been backed, so do us a favour and work with us on this.' And, in a sense, those prices were public property."

Simon Clare, now Coral's PR director, recognises that Pricewise posed an entirely new threat to the bookmakers. "I think Mark Coton's original ideas about value were anathema to bookies," says Clare. "They'd been used to punters who would focus on the most likely winner, which would be the favourite or the second favourite. Compilers used to worry far less about 16-1 or 25-1 shots because punters would rarely look beyond the top two or three in the market. If some shrewd punter, or someone who'd had the word from the stable, came in wanting to back a horse at 25-1 you could lay one bet and then cut it. Pricewise – and especially the grids in the *Racing Post* – changed that. If you're advertising prices in the paper they have to be available in the morning. In those days there was probably a stronger guarantee to hold the price so it could be a nightmare when you were top price about a Pricewise horse and an even bigger nightmare when the axe fell later in the day and it won! It heaped pressure on the compilers."

Mark Coton agrees that around the time Pricewise was launched punters were instinctively wary of outsiders. "A lot of punters at that stage had never backed a 14-1 winner in their lives," he says. "They'd never been schooled to do it." Taberna Lord, 14-1 in the morning, provided those punters with an early lesson that big-priced winners can be found and their education continued with the introduction of the price grids.

By November 1989, Coton's column was accompanied by these grids, which allowed punters to compare and contrast the prices from various bookmakers. On Saturday, November 14, there were grids for four races from Cheltenham, including the Mackeson Gold Cup. They featured early prices from, in alphabetical order, Chandler, Coomes, Coral, Dennis, Hills, Ladbrokes, Mecca and Tote. The runners were listed in racecard order, as opposed to price order as they are now, and the odds were all printed in bold type (later, only the best prices would be bolded up). The clear, user-friendly format left no hiding place for price discrepancies. Readers could see at once, for example, that Von Trappe was 8-1 with Ladbrokes for the Nicole Instruments Handicap Hurdle but just 11-2 with Chandler, or that Nos Na Gaoithe was rated a 13-2 chance by Mecca for the Allinson Bread Hurdle when Ladbrokes were offering only 9-2.

"I'm sure Mark would be the first to admit that it was easier to spot the mistakes then because it was a less sophisticated trading environment," says Alan Byrne. "Sometimes the prices stood out so much they might as well have had bells on them. The trading departments of bookmakers are far better organised now. There are still people willing to take a view on some horses but they probably don't take a view as often as tipsters and punters would like them to."

By the time of Mel Collier's breakthrough winner, Multum In Parvo in the 1990 Mackeson Gold Cup, the grids had been tweaked so that the best prices for each horse were in bold type and the best-price percentage was printed alongside the each-way terms at the bottom of each race. That format has remained the same, although the spread of bookmakers whose prices appear in the grids is subject to change, depending on advertising deals and other logistical issues.

Collier knew that Pricewise was a problematical area for most bookmakers. "It always a double-edged sword for the bookies," he says. "It created a lot of publicity for them but also a lot of hassle when they were the standout price. They'd have punters moaning that they could only get ten quid on or that they'd rung up at two minutes past nine and the price had already been cut. But once it was fully established, once it was in its pomp, I'd have lower-grade, smaller bookies ringing me up and asking for their prices to go in the grids. And I'd say to them 'do you really want to be in the Pricewise grid? If you're in there, you're going to get 300 phone calls between nine o'clock and five past nine – can you cope with that? Are your odds compilers up to it? You'll be up against the big boys – do you really want to do that? It's up to you.' Some of them then said no and some of them were just desperate to get in, presumably because they were under pressure from their own PR people."

For some bookmakers, the association with Pricewise is a real test of nerve, as Alan Byrne has witnessed: "I've had conversations with a few bookmakers when we've said 'you can take an advert on the Pricewise page of the paper every Saturday or every day when there's live racing on Channel 4. That's the place where you want to be.' And they've said 'actually, it's not the place we want to be because we don't want to get caught out.' From time to time, bookmakers say 'you know what? We should come out of the Pricewise grids because it's costing us. When we're wrong, it's costing us a lot of money.'

"Our view would be that the bookmakers need to back their trading departments. If the trading departments know what they're doing, then they should be happy to be in Pricewise. If they don't, then you shouldn't be reviewing whether or not you're in the Pricewise grids – you should be reviewing the make-up of your trading department.

"Pricewise is a great shop window for bookmakers. To take the point that

John McCririck regularly makes, it shows the amazing competitiveness of British bookmaking – the range of prices that are available and the competition in the marketplace."

Bookmakers' complaints should always be taken with a cellar or two of salt. On September 3, 2005, the *Racing Post* ran a news piece documenting Segal's amazing run of form. Tellingly, the last line of the article informed readers that "William Hill yesterday announced they are to offer early prices on every UK mainland race every day, starting this morning." Either the bookies were gluttons for punishment or they had made the cold, hard business decision that offering early prices was well worth any Pricewise-inflicted wounds.

For most punters, however, these business matters are far less intriguing than Pricewise's duel with the odds compilers. "I think it's good PR for Pricewise when Tom appears on TV for the Grand National or Derby day because he represents that battle between punters and bookmakers," says Simon Clare of Coral. "Whatever the technological advances have been over the past 25 years, that battle still exists. And with fixed-odds bookmakers – unlike the exchanges or the Tote – there is still that element of opinion in our prices. Our compiler James Knight often finds himself on the right side of Pricewise tips but that's because he thinks about racing the same way as Tom does."

Clare is aware of the pressures on Coral's odds compilers. "On a Friday, the two most important things for the compilers working on the next day's big race are to get the price of the favourite right – do they want to take it on or swerve it? – and to try and second-guess Pricewise," he says. "You're never going to avoid it completely – even if we're 12-1 about his tip and it's 16-1 elsewhere – because punters take all rates down on Pricewise horses but you hope to avoid serious injuries."

James Knight, or 'the dark Knight', as Segal cheerfully calls him, is well qualified to discuss the "battle" between Pricewise and the odds compilers. The language of war is often applied to betting – Alastair Down wrote gleefully in the *Racing Post* in 2005 that Segal had "lobbed grenades down the front of the bookies' trousers" for the previous five weeks, while Knight reveals the horses he'll be backing and laying each Saturday in a *Post* feature entitled Behind Enemy Lines.

"I've been at Coral for more than ten years," Knight says. "When I started, Mel Collier was still doing Pricewise and now, of course, it's Tom Segal but the column has always had a big effect on the way we price up Saturday races.

"We're usually happy with our prices the day before but, once we've read the Pricewise selection and maybe seen a positive quote from the trainer, we may well think again. If we're a standout price about a Pricewise horse then the vast majority of times we'll be feeling wary. It's very rare that we'll look at a Pricewise selection and say 'he's definitely got this one wrong.' Just the fact that Tom has tipped a horse is enough to move the market in its favour and there are very few occasions when we'd be happy to lay it. I think he tipped Black Spirit for the Winter Derby and we thought he'd got that wrong – we were a best-priced 14-1 and it finished fourth – but there's just a handful of examples of that happening in the last ten years.

"We really start to worry when Tom tips in something like a handicap hurdle at Kempton in January when the ground's soft. They're difficult races to price up anyway because there's such volatility in the market. A horse can be 33-1 in the morning and suddenly if Pricewise tips it and the yard fancies it, it'll be sent off at 8-1. There's no way out for the bookmakers in that situation. You can't lay something at 25-1 and then back it back at 8-1 because you'll be locking in a big loss and you're not able to lay enough of the other runners. There were a couple of Pricewise winners like that in January 2012 – Ciceron won a handicap hurdle at Sandown at 16-1 and the next week Swincombe Flame won, having been backed from 9-1 in to 9-2. I think they cost us about £350,000 each.

"The Pricewise factor is certainly built into our prices. It is always on your mind as a compiler but that's part of the challenge of the job, putting out competitive prices that we're happy to lay. We're always trying to second-guess Tom. He has a very different tipping style to Mel Collier, who loved speed figures, whereas Tom has a more intuitive feel. He'd be looking for an interesting horse that hasn't shown its full potential so when I'm looking at a race there might be two or three runners that fit the bill. I'd think 'yeah, that could be the one Tom goes for' and obviously we'd keep those two or three onside.

"There's a funny kind of relationship between me and Tom. Obviously, I'll speak to him each week to give him our prices and we'll have a chat about racing. He's a great guy – very successful but modest. There's not

Fayr Jag powers to victory in Ascot's Golden Jubilee Stakes on an expensive day for bookmakers in June 2004

a hint of arrogance about him, which is unusual in racing, I think. Most people who have their head in the form book the whole time, looking to beat the bookies, need to have a huge ego and be very single-minded but Tom's a one-off. He manages to be a fantastic tipster and a really nice guy. Although he's great fun to talk to, he can also do us a great deal of damage."

Simon Clare confirms the damage that a successful Pricewise tip can do to a bookmaker. "We took an absolute battering when Pasternak won the Cambridgeshire," he says. "Not only because of Pricewise, in that case, but also because of the big Graham Rock gamble. And the Saturday of Royal Ascot in 2004 was one of Coral's worst ever day's racing. Tom tipped Lafi to win the Wokingham and Fayr Jag for the Golden Jubilee and we were top price about both of them in the morning. Even though Tom doesn't tip multiples, when punters see one firm offering best prices about a couple of his selections, they'll take advantage and put them in a double, which proved extremely expensive for us that day."

Knight also recalls that Saturday in 2004 with some pain: "When we get a Pricewise horse wrong, it costs us significant sums. We've had some disastrous days, the worst being Lafi and Fayr Jag at Royal Ascot. We were top price about both horses and we lost well over £500,000 just on the morning punters who followed the Pricewise tips."

Graham Sharpe, the long-serving media director at William Hill, describes Pricewise as "a necessary evil. As bookmakers, we have to take our hats off to its level of consistency. It's like Frankie Dettori's magnificent seven at Ascot – it cost us millions but we had to grit our teeth and tell ourselves that it would benefit the industry in the long term. Pricewise might tip punters a headline winner but hopefully they'll fritter away the winnings on their own bets. If you're very disciplined, with a decent staking plan, then following Pricewise will be profitable, but that's not the way most punters want to play. They want to have an interest in several races a day.

"It probably irritates punters who do their homework because it ruins the price but it makes it far easier for the bone-idle punters, who will back Pricewise blind! And you'll hear the same lament from bookies because it skews the book, although it does help us in some ways. Whereas we used to be second-guessing which horse would be the serious punters' choice in a big race, now we have Pricewise as a good guide.

"I think it's important to remember that Pricewise is operating in a relatively specialised market, being in the *Racing Post*. We'll still see people following whatever Derek Thompson or Templegate in *The Sun* has tipped and others follow the tipsters in the *Mirror* or the *Star*. Pricewise is certainly the experts' expert, though. There is damage done when he tips the winner of a big race, like Papillon in the Grand National, but it's tempered by the money following tipsters in *The Sun* and the other papers. Papillon was tough but we lived to fight another day."

The arrival of Betfair has had an enormous impact on the bookmaking industry but its effect on Pricewise has been less dramatic. "You cannot argue with what Betfair has provided for punters," says Tom Segal. "It's provided them with the opportunity to back horses at backable prices and to get lots of money on those horses, which they were never able to do before.

"In terms of my job, though, it hasn't really made that much of a difference. I'm slightly different from most punters, in that I'm only playing with the traditional bookmakers and I'm only playing the day before a race. When you're doing it the day before a race, the Betfair markets haven't really evolved so they don't really play a part. Now, five minutes before the off, you look at the Betfair markets and you know at once whether your horse has got a chance, whether it's fancied or not."

The *Racing Post*'s betting editor Paul Kealy agrees with Segal's analysis. "Because the Betfair markets are quite light early in the morning, Pricewise followers will still go to the traditional bookmakers," says Kealy. "You'll see on Betfair a queue of money trying to get on the Pricewise tip from people who want to trade it but the markets on the exchanges aren't heavily traded very early in the morning."

Segal doesn't deny that life has changed since the arrival of the betting exchanges. "What Betfair probably has done is make the traditional bookies sharper," he says. "In Mark's day, he would be pointing out massive variances in price between, say, Ladbrokes and Coral. At this stage, though, because the bookies are a lot sharper, the prices are far more uniform. Without decrying other sports too much, horse racing has always been the biggest thing for bookmakers. Racing and football probably make up, I'd guess, 80 per cent of their betting so those are the sports they're going to concentrate on. It's fairly easy to price up a golf tournament – the prices are pretty much the same every week. Rory McIlroy's 7-1, Lee Westwood's 10-1 – that's just the way it is.

"But the bookmakers can't afford to slip up on racing. They'll have loads of guys working on the racing each day – good guys, Oxbridge types, proper serious odds compilers who spend all day pricing up races. Kevin Pullein [the *Racing Post*'s renowned football tipster] says that every time you have a bet, you're taking on incredibly clued-up and professional compilers and he's absolutely right. You're trying to get the better of them, which is becoming harder and harder. Because of Betfair, the traditional bookies have to attract even better people to work for them to make sure that they keep their edge in the market.

"They don't make many mistakes these days. It might look as though they do when you compare the Betfair SP to the morning prices but you have to remember that the compilers were pricing up the race 24 hours before Betfair got involved. So much more information goes into the market after that, which they couldn't have known about – information about the ground, the draw, the jockeys, and just whether or not a horse is fancied."

Coral's James Knight agrees that the betting exchanges have forced bookmakers to raise their games. "The advent of Betfair has made it harder to price up Pricewise races. In the old days if we wanted to oppose a favourite that was 2-1 everywhere else then we'd go 5-2 and if we thought it was the right call we'd lay it regardless. Now if it's the right call, the market on the exchanges will reflect that – it'll be 3-1 on Betfair and we won't see a penny for it. But if we get one wrong, people try to get as much as they can on."

Like every other punter, those playing on the betting exchanges know the value of discovering the Pricewise selections at an early stage. "The night before a big race there will be movements on the betting exchanges," says Alan Byrne. "People think they've spotted the Pricewise horse although actually it'll often be the wrong one – or it'll be one that somebody is trying to make look like the Pricewise horse.

"I suppose you do get a lot of people then piling in to back what they think is the Pricewise tip. Equally, there may be those who think 'well, he's not on a good run – I'll take my chances and lay it.' Personally, I'd rather be among the backers than the layers because, as the record shows, ultimately the layers will lose.

"Of course, the exchanges allow people who have got the early prices to trade out but in general they haven't had the same impact on Pricewise as they have on on-course bookmakers, for example. You see on-course bookmakers now who couldn't trade without seeing the Betfair prices whereas so long as Tom has a set of prices from the bookmakers he can form a view. So I don't think the exchanges have had as much of an impact on Pricewise as they might have done."

The arrival of the betting exchanges has, however, encouraged the conspiracy theories that Pricewise seems to inspire. Ever since its launch, and the accusations that Mark Coton was in league with the bookmakers to blunt the threat of hard-working value seekers, rumours have abounded. "Some people look at the firms who regularly underprice Tom's tips and think that they must be getting inside information," says John McCririck. "I'm sure that's not the case, though. It's all part of the mystique, the plotting and scheming that goes into betting."

Alan Byrne admits that "you get a whole range of conspiracy theories. People look at the prices in the grids and take a view as to which bookmaker is well informed about which horses – which firms know about particular stables. Lots of people read lots of things into the prices, not all of which should be read into them, but it adds to the intrigue."

The accessibility of Pricewise has certainly contributed to its impact on the betting industry. "From the moment I joined Coral in 1997 it was clear that Pricewise was the most influential tipping service in the country," says Simon Clare. "For a start, it was publicly available for the cost of a paper, unlike a telephone tipping line or a subscription service." John McCririck agrees: "I deplore telephone tipsters. If they knew all the winners, they wouldn't need to be advertising their tipping lines, would they? I simply cannot understand why anyone pays for them when you won't get better than Pricewise."

Graham Sharpe, Media Relations Director at Willian Hill, believes that punters' faith in the integrity of Pricewise is the key. "One interesting aspect is that it seems to be irrelevant who is actually writing Pricewise," Sharpe says. "People just see it as Pricewise and take notice of the column itself rather than the individual writer. It's become a quality brand – some people will buy something just because it says Marks & Spencer on it and, likewise, some punters will back anything that Pricewise tips. They know that whoever is writing it will have put the work in because of the profile of the column and the pressure to do well. The brand seems to transcend whichever expert has written it."

It is vital for the Pricewise "brand" that the prices advertised in the *Racing Post* are available to punters. The paper addressed this issue in March 2003 when the bookmakers whose prices featured in the grids signed up to The Punters' Charter. "When Pricewise tips a horse at early prices, what guarantee is there that you can get on at the advertised odds?" the *Post* asked. "There is nothing more galling than reading in the *Racing Post* that Pricewise tipped a 10-1 winner after you tried – and failed – to get on [...] Hopefully, The Punters' Charter will help you, the backer, know exactly where you stand."

The need for such a charter was demonstrated by the variety of bookmakers' policies. Coral's response was curt: "Coral-advertised prices will be available in betting shops until at least 10.15am" but other firms required five or six paragraphs to make their positions clear. Ladbrokes grandly announced that "while many people expect bookmakers to honour a 15-minute guarantee, we believe this is the first time that a major bookmaker has put that commitment in black and white to its customers." Victor Chandler, who described themselves as "a 24-hour trading operation", explained that "we cannot give any firm guarantee as to how long we hold early prices. It can depend on various factors, like whether the horse is 4-1 or 33-1 and whether it's the Royal Hunt Cup or a handicap chase at Market Rasen." And Bet365 defended their policy of restricting stakes on Pricewise selections. "A Pricewise tip would prove to be popular at 9am on a Saturday," the firm wrote. "Instead of laying a few lumpy bets and cutting the price at 9.01, we like to limit the stake (depending on price) to, say, £50 each-way per customer so our clients can be accommodated."

Alan Byrne understands the bookmakers' point of view: "It's difficult because if Tom Segal is in flying form, tipping 16-1 and 20-1 winners left, right and centre, then the bookmakers are having to stand up to the Charge of the Light Brigade. There's a balance to be struck. We get some bookmakers whinging about how difficult it is but we also get readers who are unhappy that they couldn't get the price. So then we have to put some pressure on the bookies and tell them that if they're not going to honour the prices, we're not going to publish the prices. That's why there have been various attempts to get some sort of guarantee that the bookmakers will lay the prices and, in general, they've been very good at saying 'right, for shop punters we'll have these rules' and so on."

"Bookmakers are wary of Pricewise tips," Paul Kealy says. "They have to control what they're laying and put limits on how much punters can have, which is reasonable. If Tom's tipped one at 25-1 then their liabilities will soon mount up even if they're only laying tenners. We introduced a charter a few years ago in which each bookmaker promised to lay the price quoted in the paper for a certain amount or a certain length of time. Hopefully they stick to that charter, although sometimes it can literally be a five-minute window and then the price is gone."

Segal remains sanguine about the arguments over prices being cut and stakes being reduced. "It's just part of the business," he says. "It's a pain in the arse for me to have people phoning up complaining about not getting on – but what can I do about it? I'm not working for Hills or Ladbrokes. I suppose I could tip loads of losers and then maybe they'd keep their prices but that's not my job. It's frustrating and I understand why punters get pissed off but there's nothing I can do about it. It's another reason why I'm not a fan of staking plans, though. I think it's a ridiculous thing to say 'have ten points on this at 6-1' because nobody in the world can get ten times their normal stake on with the bookies."

The latest version of The Punters' Charter can be found in the Tipping section of racingpost.com. The rise of internet betting and 24-hour trading has muddied the waters a little but the firms still pledge that their advertised prices will be honoured. William Hill claim that "we open betting with our prices at 5.30pm the day before the race (sometimes earlier for feature races). These are traded in retail until the shops close and all the way through the night online. Naturally, prices do fluctuate throughout the evening trading and in particular the Pricewise selections. We will always re-release advertised prices that are in print in the *Racing Post* at 9am (irrespective of shop opening time). We will endeavour to hold our prices for as long as possible."

"Early" prices seem to be getting earlier and earlier. "Betting on all Pricewise races is available from 5.30pm the previous day across all channels, and often earlier," say Ladbrokes. "These channels include our shops, online and call centre. On the morning of the Pricewise races we will offer our advertised prices to our customers for a period of 15 minutes, usually from 8.15am." And it's a case of 'you snooze, you lose' for morning punters, particularly with Paddy Power, who warn that "our prices will be available for a minimum of five minutes, for Saturdays from 8.30am, for Sunday to Friday from 9am."

Despite the inevitable complaints from punters – and bookmakers – Simon Clare of Coral believes that the culture of early prices is a significant benefit to Pricewise. "Telephone and internet betting has helped the growth of Pricewise," Clare says. "We put our prices up on the website at 8.30am. We're always keen to stand firm and hold the price – it's about customer service as much as anything. Ideally, the prices advertised in the Pricewise grid should all be available at the same time so punters aren't scrambling around to find out what time Bet365 or Hills or Ladbrokes are guaranteeing their prices till. We won't make money out of the guarantee – there will always be the arbitrage guys trying to nick a couple of quid – but we know our customers and we will always aim to offer the price to those who just want a tenner on the Pricewise tip.

"Of course we have to control liabilities but it's also important to accommodate Pricewise followers. Bookmakers often look at the the black/red, profit/loss figure on Pricewise tips but they forget that the morning rush on the internet and in the shops is great for business. It's clearly a remarkable tipping service to have survived for so long and it also promotes fixed-odds bookies' prices." Alan Byrne echoes that view: "By and large, while the bookmakers moan about it sometimes – they certainly don't like it when they're top price about a horse Tom has selected – they also see that it's a good shop window for them."

If those prices are guaranteed – whether it's for a matter of minutes, seconds or nanoseconds – then it can only be good news for punters. A *Racing Post* feature in 2011 analysed the big-race price war between traditional bookmakers as they sought to attract new customers and lure old ones back from the betting exchanges. "The bookmakers have joined the horsemen in a scramble for black type – albeit the black type they crave is the bold best price in the *Racing Post*'s Pricewise tables," wrote reporter Tom Kerr. "In July, morning prices for several of the biggest Saturday races produced best-priced under-rounds, meaning punters who got on early could back every horse in the race and still return a profit. The Coral-Eclipse on July 2 had an under-round of 93 per cent, the King George VI and Queen Elizabeth Stakes was 94 per cent, the Nassau 95 per cent and the Sussex Stakes 99 per cent."

The article quoted tipster and punter Eddie Fremantle, who agreed that "for the ordinary punter on the face of it things are very good. Obviously, if you are following a successful tipping service like Pricewise there might be problems getting on at the advertised prices, but in the Pricewise boxes on Saturday there was one race at 106 per cent, one at 104 and all the rest were 102. At those percentages it is difficult not to get value."

This kind of debate about value demonstrates the evolution of punters' thinking over the past 25 years. Since Mark Coton's day, when gamblers simply wanted to be told the most likely winner and 'value' was regarded as a quirky sideline of betting, bookmakers and punters have become more savvy, more sophisticated and more aware of value.

Simon Clare has observed this change during his time at Coral. "There are distinct types of punter," he says. "There's still a group who just want to bet. They don't really mind what they're betting on and they tend to zone in on favourites. But Pricewise has helped to create a more intelligent, more analytical breed of punters who are willing to use the information on the internet, look at the different approaches of the tipsters in the

Racing Post – not just Pricewise, but Trading Post and Spotlight and Trends. These punters are more price-sensitive, partly because it's so easy to watch the market on Oddschecker or Betfair. Before the internet you'd be waiting ten minutes for the Teletext pages to flick over before you could compare Ladbrokes' prices with Victor Chandler's and by the time you'd worked out who was top price it would have gone anyway!"

The technology may have changed – the digital switchover has sounded the death knell for Teletext – but the poacher/gamekeeper relationship between punters and bookmakers remains the same. And, whether the bets have been laid over the counter, on the phone or through the website, the bookies feel the same sense of dread when a well-backed Pricewise horse hits the front with 150 yards left to run in a big handicap.

THE READERS' PERSPECTIVE

WHEN A GAMBLER backs a winner, it is entirely down to his skill and judgement. When he backs a loser, it's the fault of the jockey, the trainer, the clerk of the course, the alignment of the stars or the so-called mate who gave him the tip. Racing punters are not renowned for their patience, as anybody who has ever set foot in a betting shop will know, so Pricewise's lofty reputation among the betting public has been hard-earned.

The very fact that Pricewise appears in the *Racing Post* means that it is being judged by the most passionate and informed racing fans in the country. Pricewise is "the expert's expert", as Graham Sharpe said in the previous chapter. Lee Mottershead, writing in the *Post* in 2005, described the column as "punters' most prized asset" and Francis Kelly also regards it as a luxury item for the paper's readers. "It's the hardest job in the world, setting yourself up as a tipster, but Mark, Mel and Tom have all been absolutely superb," Kelly says. "And the *Racing Post* has been fortunate in that we could afford the luxury of Pricewise. No other newspaper has tipsters of that calibre because their racing guys are expected to write reports, news stories, features and then do a few tips."

Alan Byrne, the *Racing Post*'s chief executive and editor-in-chief, believes that hard graft is behind Pricewise's consistent service to the *Racing Post*'s readers. "All of us as punters kid ourselves that we approach racing with a great rigour but Mark, Mel and Tom actually do have that approach to their homework and their tipping," says Byrne. "Obviously, that works to the benefit of the column and the readers, while showing up the rest of us for our lack of rigour!"

It is hard to avoid the language of religion when writing about successful tipsters. Those punters who regularly back Pricewise tips are "followers" – or even "disciples" – and keeping the faith is vital, whether the column is drenched in milk and honey or wandering alone in the wilderness. A tipster without followers is like a shepherd without a flock and this chapter will explore the relationship between Pricewise and its disciples.

When the column was launched, Mark Coton encountered a hostile public. Irate punters accused him of killing the goose that laid the golden egg by tipping off bookmakers about the vast price discrepancies that were available at the time. But Pricewise's instant impact – three winners in its first three weeks, at advised prices of 14-1, 8-1 and 13-2 – soon elicited a more positive response from readers.

"I was able to get some kind of feedback because there were a few people I knew who followed the column," Coton says. "My window cleaner, for example, backed my tips with a few of his mates. Funnily enough, if I'd tipped one at 6-1 and it started at 4-1 and won, people liked it but if I put up one at 14-1 they wouldn't back it. Once it got beyond 10-1 or 12-1 they weren't interested in it, simply because it was "too big" a price. Just going on the small sample of people I knew, there seemed to be a price threshold which was really quite low.

"If I'd tipped a winner at 14-1 or 16-1 I'd see my window cleaner in the cafe and think 'well, I'm going to get a cup of tea out of this' but he and his mates wouldn't have been on it – they hadn't fancied it because it was 14-1. Now, of course, Pricewise has a lot of followers and people automatically back the tips because they trust Tom and they know it works. But for me, Pricewise was about tips like Gold Seam which was 7-2 in to 2-1 – they were the ones that people wanted."

Coton's approach attracted readers who were serious about betting and keen to improve their punting habits. One, a former City trader-turned-professional punter, recalls that "punting had always been a serious hobby for me and in the early years I followed Mark Coton's Pricewise column religiously. It appealed to me because it tackled the most competitive races. Not everybody wants to play in those races but they attract serious punters because they're the most difficult ones for bookmakers to price up."

One reason for the success of Pricewise is the simple enthusiasm for racing that Coton, Mel Collier and Tom Segal convey in their columns. Segal has a clear idea of the kind of racing fan at whom Pricewise is aimed. "I've always thought that Pricewise is for the man in the betting shop," he says. "It's not tailored for massive punters like Harry Findlay. It's for the guy who wants to have a fiver each-way in the shop on a Saturday and if it wins he can pick up 50 quid and go out for a curry with his mates instead of going home to the missus. Some people take Pricewise too seriously but that's what I've always thought it was about.

"I never get mail from people saying I'm having a terrible run and I never get mail from people saying I'm having a brilliant run. Most people don't take it too seriously. I go to Ireland quite a lot because they like racing more than English people do, generally, and when you go over there you realise that most people just want to have a bit of fun with their betting.

"The *Racing Post* sponsored a race on Irish National day so I went to that and people came up to say hello because I do some Cheltenham previews over there and so on. Willie Mullins invited me to his yard and Ruby Walsh came and said hello but it's a bit different in England. I go racing quite rarely in England – I go to Cheltenham during the Festival occasionally and to the *Racing Post* Trophy at Doncaster – but I don't really get much attention. The odd person might come up and say 'how are you doing?' or 'you're useless' but it's very rare."

Mel Collier doesn't remember being swamped, either by bouquets or by brickbats, during his many years as Pricewise. "There would be the odd bottle of champagne if I'd tipped a big winner," he says. "I'd get phone calls and some really lovely letters from readers, thanking me and praising me up and saying they'd pay for a holiday, but I suspect any negative feedback would be filtered out."

Collier has held on to most of the letters that he received from grateful readers. Some, like this one from December 2000, are polite but brief: "Dear Mr Collier. My father and I would like to show our appreciation for your great expertise, which has turned two losing punters into winners. I wish us continued success." In June 2001, another correspondent wrote, more familiarly: "Dear Melvyn, Just a note to say thank you for turning me into a winning punter. The hardest thing is getting the bets on at the price and the best is watching them run well."

The announcement that Collier would be handing over the Pricewise job inspired several letters from readers. "As someone who has followed your advice assiduously over the last three or four years I hear the news of your departure from the *Racing Post* with mixed feelings," one wrote. "If you are indeed going to run a tipping service then, from my point of view, life suddenly becomes easier – the mornings will be less of a battle with the early-price merchants because presumably the traffic will be easier. I hope however that you will maintain the same principles of 'value' selections with a low strike-rate at good prices. I am rapidly realising that that is

Newmill: one of two 33-1 ante-post winners for Tom Segal at Cheltenham in 2006

the only successful long-term strategy. Please keep me informed of any service you will be running and if you do decide to cultivate your garden, thank you for your excellent help over the years."

Perhaps the response that epitomises the affection felt by readers for Pricewise – as well as fulfilling Tom Segal's advice that betting should, above all, be fun – came in the form of a letter to the editor in November 2000. "Dear Sir," it began, "I feel utterly compelled to write to you after once more witnessing the pure magic of Pricewise (Melvyn Collier). This man has given me so much satisfaction and financial reward for the mere price of a *Racing Post*! Today, for instance, I was able to have £10 on an 8-1 shot, £5 each-way on a 40-1 shot and a £1 reverse exacta on the Hennessy – a return of approx. £290 for a £22 stake. I wonder how he stands this year on a £1 level stake? His knowledge of the form book and ability to race-read the video footage surpass any other tipster. I'm surprised that Channel 4's 'Morning Line' doesn't employ him. He could run it on his own! With far better results! Finally, please give this amazing man my heartfelt thanks and protect him from possible hit-men from Corals, Ladbrokes and Hills!"

The £5 and £10 punter – or the £1 reverse exacta punter – may be Pricewise's main constituency but the column is respected by professional gamblers too. The professional punter quoted earlier in this chapter believes that the Pricewise approach captures the essence of profitable betting. "I used to work as a City trader and when I was made redundant in 2005 I decided I'd try to go full-time on Betfair, mainly betting on racing and tennis," he says. "I realised that if you knew which way the price was going you could have bigger bets and then lay them off without risk. The nature of punting seriously is finding the horse that shortens in the market, which is what Mark Coton was doing all those years ago.

"Mel Collier and then Tom Segal have taken Pricewise to another level. It's impossible for serious punters to get on at the best prices these days but Tom's tips also have a significant effect on the Betfair market. If something is 12-1 with the independents and 10-1 with Ladbrokes in the morning then it will probably be trading at 8-1 or 8.5-1 on Betfair. I certainly have ultimate respect for Tom as one of the greatest judges to walk the earth."

That accolade is echoed by Patrick Veitch, the professional gambler who – according to the title of his autobiography – is regarded by bookmakers as Enemy Number One. "I sometimes wonder what it would be like to have a World Series of Horse Racing Gambling, with a titanic prize fund to rival the World Series of Poker," Veitch says. "I doubt if such a plan could ever work, but if it did happen I could safely say that Tom Segal would be the person I'd least like to be drawn against in a heat, and the person most likely to have me burning the midnight oil in preparation."

Veitch has made a living from betting on racing and Pricewise has helped at least one *Racing Post* reader get a glimpse of that lifestyle. The reader wishes to remain anonymous but is "keen to share my thoughts on something which has influenced my life so much in the past ten years or so." He first noticed the column, fortunately enough, on Grand National day in the year 2000. "I discovered Pricewise when Mel Collier was still doing it," he says. "The first Pricewise horse I backed was Papillon to win the Grand National. I just had a little bet on it and it escalated from there.

"For me, though, the glory days came when Tom Segal took over. I didn't follow him immediately – I think his first few months were a bit shaky and I just watched his tips for at least a year without backing them. Then he had a big treble at Royal Ascot, including Attache at 33-1, so I thought I'd better start following him after that."

The need for a tipster to win over his readers is a common theme and those who were convinced by Segal early on have been rewarded handsomely over the years. "I only work for half the year now because of Pricewise," this lucky reader admits. "Tom has been financing that for the last few years! Back in the days when I could get on I'd be backing his tips for £250 or £300 a point. I'd had £250 each-way on Newmill and Star de Mohaison at 33-1 ante-post the day they both won at Cheltenham. It sounds great, winning 20 grand in a day, but obviously part of that goes to cover the losers. If you can't deal with the losing runs then Pricewise probably isn't for you.

"I used to follow Henry Rix too but he'd give four bets at midday and it was a real struggle to get them all on before the prices went. At least with Pricewise you'd get 15 minutes' grace in the shops. I realised that Pricewise was the one and gradually increased my stakes until it got to £300 per point. One year I think I ended up 150 points in profit, which was amazing.

"There were so many good days. I had £100 each-way on Tominator at 50-1 in the Northumberland Plate and I backed Edinburgh Knight at 33-1 on Champions Day at Ascot. There was Numbersixvalverde in the National and Sir Percy and Authorized ante-post for the Derby. I think Authorized was tipped at 8-1 and went off at 5-4."

That level of success has inevitably attracted the attention of the bookmakers. "I struggle to get a bet on these days," the reader laments. "The bookies do my head in, offering a fiver or whatever on the Pricewise selections. You can't really blame them because it must have been costing them fortunes but I've had to cut my stakes right back. I get what I can on and do a bit on Betfair, but then you have to factor the commission in to that, so for me the golden days are probably over.

"I'm not really looking for value bets – I've just got so much faith in Pricewise. It's all about Tom. If he left then I wouldn't follow his replacement blind. They'd have to prove themselves and earn my faith."

This particular case study of a Pricewise follower may be an unusual one. Tom Segal's "man in the betting shop" certainly wouldn't be backing Pricewise tips to £300 a point but it demonstrates the remarkable confidence that readers have in the column's reliability and results.

Niall Davison from Belfast is also a huge admirer of Segal. Davison, however, sees Pricewise as more than just a cash cow – it is an education in punting. "Pricewise has played a massive part in my betting and my whole approach to betting over the last five years," he says. And, as the tuition fees are no more than the price of a newspaper, this education represents excellent value.

"I got into racing quite late," Davison says. "I'd always like betting on football and golf, mainly accumulators on the football. In 2007 someone I met at work told me about a system they had that used Postdata and the tipsters' selection box in the *Racing Post*. I soon realised that the system was a load of crap but by then I'd started reading the *Post* daily and got the racing bug."

Davison's background in football betting meant that he was used to regular, albeit short-priced, winners. Like Coton's readers, who were wary of backing a horse at 14-1 just because it was 14-1, he was happier backing the racing equivalent of a Manchester United home win. "Because I was used to having accas on the football, I started out looking for short-priced horses to put in doubles and trebles," he says. "I'd be backing these favourites and they'd get done on the line by some 12-1 shot and Alastair Down on Channel 4 would say 'congratulations to Tom Segal – he put this one up at 20-1 in the *Racing Post* this morning.' And I thought 'who is this Segal guy?'

"I'd been reading a few books about betting and I realised that I needed to find bigger-priced winners rather than just 6-4 or 7-4 favourites. And when I started reading the Pricewise columns I saw at once that Tom knew what he was talking about so I began to follow him in around 2008."

Davison is far from a passive Pricewise follower, however. He sees Segal as a tutor and is as interested in the reasoning behind a tip as he is in the result. "It sounds strange considering I've never met Tom but he's almost become a mentor to me in terms of betting," he says. "I don't just read Pricewise for the tips – I'm interested in how he comes to his conclusions and he's given me so much good advice over the years. I think I'm a far better punter now, thanks to him, because his ideas have helped me look at a race and draw my own conclusions."

Davison, like Mel Collier, is a believer in the value of other people's opinions and he keeps an eye on various other tipsters. "I've always looked at the tipsters' selection box, just to see what *The Sun* or the *Telegraph* have napped and I think they're all good in their own way," he says. "Hugh Taylor on the At The Races website is a genius and I'll always listen to what Steve Mellish has to say on the television but it was soon clear to me that Tom Segal was the man! I don't understand why anyone calls tipping lines when you've got Pricewise in the paper for £2.20 every Saturday."

While the first reader quoted in this chapter was quite happy to take Segal's word that a horse was a 'value' bet, Davison is a more price-sensitive punter. "I'm certainly more aware of the importance of value in my betting now," he says. "It's hard to actually explain value but when I'm looking at the five-day decs, I'll have an idea of which will be the Pricewise races, which handicaps Tom's likely to tip on, and then I'll look again the night before and see if I can work out which horse he'll tip.

"I like the way he keeps it simple. There was a line in 'Luck' [the ill-fated HBO television series set around a California racetrack] where someone said 'I'm not handicapping the horse, I'm handicapping the trainer' and that reminded me of Tom's approach. He's very strong on trainer form and trends. Whereas someone like Hugh Taylor often goes for the eye-catchers, the horses that were unlucky last time out, Tom tends to look at it from a different angle.

"My favourite ever Pricewise tip was Final Approach to win the MCR Hurdle at Leopardstown in January 2011. I've kept that day's column and it began: 'Have you ever met anyone who has skinned a cat? I certainly haven't but I'm reliably informed there is more than one way to do it. Similarly, there are many different ways to approach winner-finding but one I've never used, until today, is owner watch.' Final Approach's form was nothing special but Tom had spotted that its owner was the managing director of the race sponsors so Willie Mullins may well have lined it up for the race. He tipped it at 14-1 and it pissed up at 6-1!"

Segal's knowledge of – and respect for – racing in Ireland sets him apart from many British journalists and tipsters, which is something that Davison appreciates. "Tom's a great follower of Irish form and that has always impressed me," he says. "Even living in Belfast, I find it hard to get a handle on the handicap system down south – personally, I follow the British racing far more closely – but Tom seems to know all about the Irish horses that go over to England. It's an angle that he has over other British-based tipsters. He quickly latched on to David Marnane's horses, for example, and he tipped up Santo Padre in the Portland Handicap and Dandy Boy in the Victoria Cup, both of which won at big prices."

After Dandy Boy's success in May 2010 – advised by Segal at 25-1 – Marnane told the *Racing Post*: "We were saying 'bet you Pricewise will pick Dandy when the weights come out.' We didn't see a *Racing Post* before getting on the plane to Ascot in the morning, but we got a text saying he was in to 16-1 and knew he must have been the Pricewise selection. When I see judges like Pricewise and Gerald Delamere put up my horses it certainly vindicates the trip. I was even called astute. Obviously they've never met me!"

Segal's regard for the trainer meant that he was kicking himself after Dandy Boy landed another huge prize, winning the Wokingham at Royal Ascot in 2012. He wrote afterwards that he had ignored one of his "golden rules" (not a phrase that he uses lightly) – namely, always back David Marnane's horses in big-field sprint handicaps.

All the lessons and hints gleaned from Pricewise would be worthless without winners and Davison has enjoyed several profitable days. "I've mentioned that Final Approach is my favourite Pricewise tip but there are plenty of other good memories," he says. "I was having a terrible day at Cheltenham in 2010 – I'd had a big bet on Get Me Out Of Here which was touched off by Menorah (a Pricewise tip that I hadn't backed) and there were another couple of near misses. I was having a stinker until I remembered that Tom had tipped A New Story in the cross-country chase. I hadn't taken the race seriously but I had £15 each-way at 40-1 so it saved the whole day and set me up for the rest of the week. I was watching it in a bar and ended up hugging some bald guy who had backed A New Story on Betfair!

"The next year at Cheltenham I'd ignored Tom's ante-post tip on Al

Tominator storms to victory in the 2011 Northumberland Plate, having been advised at 50-1 by Segal

Ferof in the Supreme Novices' – I just couldn't have it at all – so I was kicking myself when that won. I'd also felt that Captain Chris was a poor selection in the very next race but I'd backed it at 16-1, just in case. I backed Tominator at 50-1 for the Northumberland Plate although unfortunately I was keeping my stakes small at the time so only had a fiver each-way. You can't complain about a 50-1 winner, though!"

Pricewise's influence on Davison's betting extends to days and races when the column doesn't appear in the *Racing Post*. "I definitely try to use Tom's mindset in my own betting," he says. "I aim to approach racing 'the Tom Segal way' if you like. I record all my bets and I've been in profit for the last three years, partly through following Pricewise and partly through my own study.

"The best bet I've had was Son Of Flicka to win the Coral Cup at the 2012 Cheltenham Festival. I'd been watching replays of Cheltenham the year before when it ran a good race but it had rubbish form on soft ground since then. The day before the race it was the complete outsider at 66-1 and I had £15 each-way on it. The money came for it on Wednesday morning and I went in again, getting whatever the bookies would let me have on. It won at 16-1 and it was my most satisfying bet because I'd worked it out myself – and I'd told a few mates that the horse was way overpriced."

Davison's Son Of Flicka gamble confirmed him as a model student of the Pricewise school. As a frustrated Segal pointed out in Chapter Five, "it was the type of horse I could have found." In this instance, though, the apprentice managed to outwit the master.

Winners such as Son Of Flicka have given Davison the confidence to back his own judgement. "If Tom left Pricewise I wouldn't follow whoever took over blind," he says. "That's partly because I feel I'm good enough now to do my own work on a race. My motto and my advice to all my friends before any of the big meetings – Cheltenham or Ascot or the Grand National – is 'have your own opinion but have Tom Segal's too.' It sounds a bit cheesy but it's the truth – and it's definitely helped me become a better punter."

While Mark Coton and Mel Collier received a smattering of feedback – whether it be an abusive phone call or an effusive letter – Segal, operating in the era of Twitter, faces an absolute deluge of opinion. Like the Queen and various Premier League footballers, he chooses to steer clear of the social networking site but on big racedays his tips are a hot topic for racing-minded sections of the Twitterati.

He made a fleeting appearance on Twitter for a Q & A session for the *Racing Post* in July 2012, when he was asked, among other things, if he thought Camelot would beat Frankel, who would win The Open at Royal Lytham and, most importantly, whether his surname "is pronounced like the film star or like the bird?" "It's like the bird," he confirmed to a nation on the edge of its collective seat. "Never been called the film star way until I came to the *Racing Post*."

"Does the abuse you get when things don't go your way question your method or approach to how you pick your selections?" one reader asked, to which Segal responded "Don't hear any of it. Don't have a Twitter account or read forums..." And another inquisitor wished to know whether he had "ever been tempted just to throw out a no-hoper and watch the bookies squirm at the thought of a 150-1 shot?" Ever the professional, Segal replied, "No, I tip what I fancy. There are a lot of people who say my tips are no-hopers!"

After a juicy double on the second day of Glorious Goodwood in 2012, Twitter users were swift to hail Pricewise. "Tom Segal is a legend," wrote one fan. "Two of his tips came in today, 28-1 and 14-1. That's just paid for my holiday." "Tip of the cap to Tom Segal today," a deferential admirer wrote while others declared "Tom Segal is well and truly back"; "Tom Segal is an absolute guru!"; "Mr Pricewise Tom Segal is unreal"; and, a little alarmingly, "Tom Segal, I love you!"

One deft ironist of the Twittersphere was conspicuous by his silence, however. The day before Segal struck at Goodwood, this user had tweeted, "More top tipping from peerless Pricewise Tom Segal. No winners from three selections now this week. Lay, lay, lay all his selections." As Alan Byrne noted in the previous chapter, those who choose to oppose Pricewise selections on a regular basis must be prepared for some very expensive days. Fortunately, as the Twitter response to Segal's Goodwood double demonstrates, many punters still have the utmost faith in Pricewise.

WINNERS, WINNERS, WINNERS

The hype surrounding Pricewise had reached fever pitch after eight consecutive winning Saturdays in the summer of 2005. Ashkal Way, tipped by Tom Segal at 13-2, stretched that sequence to nine.

LIKE ANY TIPPING SERVICE, Pricewise's survival is entirely dependent on its results. This chapter focuses on some of the winners which helped to establish and maintain the column's influence on British and Irish racing. It is by no means a comprehensive list of Pricewise winners but, using extracts from the original tipping previews as well as memories from Mark Coton, Mel Collier and Tom Segal, it revisits a selection of the column's greatest successes.

TABERNA LORD (SANDOWN) – FEBRUARY 7, 1987

Pricewise began life on page 23 of the *Racing Post*, inauspiciously nestled between the Sandown form and an advertisement displaying The Turf Accountant Bob Menzies' prices for the afternoon's Five Nations rugby international between Ireland and England.

Despite its lowly position in the paper's pecking order, the new column could hardly be accused of hiding its light under a bushel. An introductory panel explained that "PriceWise is more than a tipping service. It aims to highlight the top-value bets of the day, the ones the professionals will be backing. This unique feature will concentrate on the races on which big bookmakers are offering 'early prices'." Anticipating The Punters' Charter, the panel concluded: "Subject to fluctuation, these prices are available from 9.30am onwards for credit and deposit account holders, and from opening time in the betting shops."

The first Pricewise column started in no-nonsense fashion. "Taberna Lord is outstanding value at 14-1 with Corals and Ladbrokes for the Tote Jackpot Handicap Hurdle (1.30) at Sandown today," Coton wrote. "Also available at 12-1 with Hills and Mecca, but as low as 10-1 with the Tote, Taberna Lord looks the pick of this competitive handicap on his form last season."

This was what Coton describes as "giving them a form angle" – a nod to the more traditional approach to tipping – but his main focus was on the market itself. Had Taberna Lord drifted from 14-1 to 25-1, it would have been a crushing – and perhaps fatal – blow to Pricewise's credibility. In fact, the Jim Wilson-trainer hurdler was backed in to 8-1 and won comfortably. Jockey Luke Harvey – whose booking, Coton wrote, "looks highly significant" – shared his memories of the race with *Racing Post* readers in 2007.

Harvey, then a conditional jockey but now better known as a broadcaster, said: "I'm proud to have a place in the history of Pricewise which, as every punter knows, has become a tipping phenomenon. I remember the race very well. I got the horse as a spare ride at Wincanton on Boxing Day where he ran adequately, and the next time over three miles, I gave him too much to do and he was a real eye-catcher, running on like crazy. He was well-in at the weights at Sandown and, watching a replay later, the commentator had plainly backed the horse because, having been held up at the back, he said 'Taberna Lord is making ground – about time too.' He absolutely hacked up and everyone joined in the punt."

According to the 1986/87 edition of *Chasers & Hurdlers*: "Taberna Lord slammed thirteen opponents in the Tote Jackpot Hurdle at Sandown in February, going clear between the last two flights to win by eight lengths from Vino Festa. It was an impressive performance."

Pricewise (or PriceWise, as it was initially billed) was off the mark and Monday's *Racing Post* carried the first of many celebratory puffs, complete with a somewhat clunky pun. Under the headline "Taberna a Wise cracker" was a rag out of Coton's tip, captioned "WHAT A WINNER: Our new feature PriceWise emphasises the morning value at 14-1."

"Taberna Lord was the business at Sandown on Saturday and *Racing Post* readers knew all about it," the puff continued. "The 8-1 winner was napped by Spotlight and Soothsayer, but that is only half the picture. PriceWise, Mark Coton's new feature, highlighted the value of the 14-1 morning price." Not content with nailing a well-backed winner first time out, Coton had also identified Vino Festa as the main danger to Taberna Lord. The 12-1 chance finished second, giving the more audacious punters among the *Racing Post* readership "a near 90-1 forecast."

Mel Collier believes Pricewise benefited greatly from being able to say "we told you to back so-and-so at 12-1 or 14-1" and the response to Taberna Lord's victory should have caught the attention of those readers who hadn't spotted the inaugural column in the depths of Saturday's paper. For those who had read Coton's first offering, it was the perfect start to a new era of tipping.

NEBLIN (NEWBURY) & RED ROCKY (CHEPSTOW) – FEBRUARY 14 & FEBRUARY 21, 1987

Taberna Lord had got Pricewise off to a flyer but there was still a sense of suspicion surrounding the new enterprise. The only way to win over the sceptics was to keep tipping winners and Coton obliged, picking Neblin and Red Rocky at decent prices on the following two Saturdays.

"Nibble at Neblin!" was the headline for the second Pricewise column and Coton wrote that the 8-1 shot could "land an old-fashioned coup in today's Tote Gold Trophy at Newbury. The ex-Irish gelding was unfavourably handicapped in his home country, but new connections could hardly believe their eyes when the weights for today's contest were announced."

However, Neblin's victory under Stan Moore wasn't a perfect Pricewise tip. Coton was forced to admit that, in this instance, he was not ahead of the game. "Those 'in the know' have snapped up all prices from 20-1 ante-post," he wrote "but Neblin looks to have everything in his favour today and still makes plenty of appeal at the morning price."

Pricewise had grabbed some great value on the race, though. "The one the ante-post layers want beaten today is Jamesmead," Coton wrote. "David Elsworth's six-year-old was recommended at 33-1 in these columns last Saturday, but is only 14-1 now after sustained backing all week." That particular gamble wasn't landed although Coton was only a year out – Jamesmead returned to Newbury to win the race in 1988.

Chasers & Hurdlers documented that the Tote Gold Trophy was won "by the gambled-on 10-1 second-favourite Neblin, who'd been quoted at 33-1 in the early ante-post lists [...] They went a cracking gallop, and a number of leading fancies began to struggle in the soft going a long way from home." Neblin, held up shrewdly, stayed on to beat Mrs Muck by two-and-a-half lengths.

Coton had made a stunning start and his column was rewarded with a new logo which, in a classic 1980s touch, replaced the two 'E's in 'Pricewise' with pound signs. However, its long-term prospects depended on the bookmakers' willingness to provide early prices. In the following Saturday's column, Coton reported that "there is a distinct lack of enthusiasm in the ante-post departments of the major bookmakers about today's racing. Newcastle's Eider Chase (2.15) is the only race covered by all five big firms and Ladbrokes and Mecca have limited their early price betting to this marathon."

Fortunately, one bookmaker was prepared to put their head above the parapet. "Hills are the only firm to bet early on a tricky-looking Gwent Hurdle and their list is well worth studying," Coton wrote. His interest in this particular contest was partly because "there is a notoriously weak market at Chepstow" so morning punters could snap up great value about a fancied horse before the price collapsed. "The one that catches my eye is Red Rocky at 13-2," Coton declared. "Jenny Pitman's charge skated in at Sandown last November and is entitled to be favourite on that form. He will be fresh after a two-month absence and is well worth an interest at the Hills price."

Red Rocky won by three lengths from Miss Nero, completing a hat-trick for the newly-launched column, but Coton was dismayed by its SP of 10-1. "It was a failure," he says because, although he had read the race correctly, the market hadn't moved in the direction he'd anticipated. It is hard to imagine a horse tipped by Tom Segal drifting in the market – especially if he'd had good-priced winners on the previous two Saturdays – but in the early days, as Red Rocky proved, Pricewise didn't wield the power that it now does. There was a plunge horse in the weak market at Chepstow but it was Bardsey, who finished third having been backed from 10-1 into 100-30.

The *Racing Post* got round the drift by quoting the SPs, rather than the advised prices, of Coton's first three winners on Monday's front page. "8-1, 10-1, 10-1 – that's the priceless PriceWise sequence over the last three Saturdays," the paper boasted, beneath stories about Michael Dickinson's departure to train in America and "Britain's most flamboyant owner" Terry Ramsden weighing up a bid for the Kentucky Derby favourite, Capote.

Taberna Lord, Neblin and Red Rocky had started to win over the doubters although some still claimed that the winners were just beginner's luck. Coton was far from satisfied, however, and he was determined to improve his analysis of the market to ensure that there were no further 'failures' such as the 10-1 winner Red Rocky.

BEAU RANGER (CHELTENHAM) – NOVEMBER 14, 1987

"A proper horse in a proper race and I'd told everybody to have a proper bet." That's how Coton describes Beau Ranger's win in the Mackeson Gold Cup – the moment when he started to believe that Pricewise had established itself.

Coton's ante-post Mackeson preview was carried on the front page the Wednesday before the race and there was no disguising his enthusiasm for Martin Pipe's contender. "Very Promising bids for his second Mackeson triumph at Cheltenham on Saturday," he wrote, "but the pick of the handicap in the first big race of the jumps season is Beau Ranger. At the 10-1 on offer with Corals, Dennis and the Tote, he looks outstanding ante-post value."

The Timeform purists couldn't have argued with the reasoning behind Coton's tip. "A winner of seven races in the 1984/85 season and conqueror of Wayward Lad at Liverpool the following year, Beau Ranger was asked to concede 1lb to Very Promising in the Mackeson last year, yet is set to receive 26lb on Saturday. He was well below form for much of last season but appeared to come right back to his best for new trainer Martin Pipe when second to Dudie at Sandown Park ten days ago. Beau Ranger raced with the zest that enabled him to land the Kennedy Construction Chase over course and distance three years ago, jumping well for Peter Scudamore and only being caught close to home in a particularly fast-run race."

By the morning of the race, Beau Ranger was vying for favouritism with Very Promising, Summons and Tickite Boo. "Readers of Wednesday's ante-post Pricewise will know this column's loyalties lie with Beau Ranger, although the morning 7-1 lacks the appeal of the 10-1 offered then," Coton wrote in Saturday's Pricewise. "Martin Pipe's nine-year-old is sure to run well off his favourable handicap mark and will like the soft ground."

The 1987/88 edition of *Chasers & Hurdlers* set the scene. The Mackeson, it wrote, "had a particularly open look about it: 4-1 the field they bet, the previous year's winner Very Promising starting favourite. But the race turned into a procession. Neither the favourite nor anything else had the slightest chance with Beau Ranger, who ran them into the ground, jumping boldly and cleanly." Mark Perrett's mount finished 15 lengths clear of runner-up Gee-A – a proper winning margin for a proper horse in a proper race.

Monday's *Racing Post* featured a rag out of the Beau Ranger tip, which it called "a 10-1 ante-post coup for followers of Mark Coton's front-page Pricewise last Wednesday." Pricewise had arrived.

NASHWAN (NEWMARKET & EPSOM) – MAY 6, 1989 & JUNE 7, 1989

Timeform's *Racehorses of 1989* described how "in the spring and summer the name Nashwan blazed like a comet through the British racing scene"

The incomparable Nashwan wins the 1989 Derby for Dick Hern, Willie Carson and Mark Coton

but Pricewise's association with the all-conquering three-year-old had started in December 1988. Mark Coton's memories of Nashwan "are as fresh as a sea breeze" and he is happy to revisit that glorious spring and summer.

"There are certain horses you had better be ready for when they come along, because they won't be coming again," says Coton. "Nashwan was one of those horses. It's probably fair to say that I used to bore my colleagues rigid with my devotion to Dick Hern's horses and to Nashwan in particular.

"Arguably, there wasn't much in the way of value at 16-1 when I tipped him for the 1989 Derby in an impromptu ante-post piece towards the end of the previous year. You could have made a case for a dozen or so on form or pedigree or profile, but when it comes down to it – to the ones that matter – it is a question of belief rather than calculation, faith rather than figures.

"My faith in Dick Hern's horses had been shaken to the sub-strata after Unfuwain's defeat in the 1988 Derby, especially as he'd been backed from

40-1 in to 9-4 shortly before the race. It was restored, however, when a flamboyant young chestnut colt seemed to gallop in another dimension when successful on his Newbury debut in August and again in a small race at Ascot in October."

Nashwan's performances as a two-year-old were enough to inspire Coton's "impromptu" ante-post Derby tip but a training setback threatened to disrupt the colt's three-year-old season. He was considered an unlikely runner in the 2,000 Guineas, not having had a prep race, and Timeform recalled that "odds of 40-1 were available about Nashwan for the Guineas a month before the race."

Amidst this uncertainty, Coton found himself in the right place at the right time. "News came through early in 1989 that the Major was to aim Nashwan at the 2,000 Guineas (the information was generously passed on by Brough Scott, who had recently visited the great man at West Ilsley). I should probably have digested it for a couple of hours and then told them to hold the front page because he was 33-1 for Newmarket when he was quoted at all. But I'd been boring them senseless for years with my devotion to Hern's horses and, anyway, it seemed too good to be true. He couldn't win both the Guineas and the Derby, could he?"

According to Timeform, "news of Nashwan's sparkling work" spread quickly and "he virtually monopolised the ante-post betting in the week before the race" before being sent off a 3-1 favourite.

"Nashwan won imperiously from the front at Newmarket, seeing off all-comers with that rich, raking stride," Coton remembers. "He was 'like a panther', said the Major, unusually voluble before the world's media in the unsaddling enclosure afterwards, dismissing inquiries about the suitability of trip and track at Epsom as if it was an absurdity of the grossest kind to be harbouring doubts in the presence of a horse as fabulous as this."

After his decisive victory in the Guineas, Coton was certain that Nashwan would complete the double. "Like the Major, I knew he'd win the Derby, in the same way that supporters of Camelot probably knew it in 2012, only Nashwan wasn't being scrubbed along two furlongs out, looking momentarily in trouble. He sauntered home with that magnificent stride, power and grace combined."

The Timeform analysis of the Derby performance was equally awestruck: "Given three or four backhanders, Nashwan opened out in breathtaking style, drawing further and further away inside the final furlong to win by an official margin of five lengths." The runner-up was Clive Brittain's Terimon – a 500-1 shot, sadly not advised each-way by Pricewise.

Coton may have been concerned that the ante-post 16-1 about Nashwan for the Derby didn't represent genuine value but nobody was complaining after the 5-4 favourite's emphatic win at Epsom. Coton himself estimated in his book *One Hundred Hints For Better Betting* that he had pulled off "a £20,000 coup" on Nashwan's two Classic wins. He felt understandably drained.

"Afterwards, I felt I needed grounding amidst a swell and surge of emotion," he recalls. "I left the track early, before the start of the next race and sat empty-eyed on the top deck of the bus back to Surbiton, staring at the comings and goings at street level below: shoppers hauling heavy bags back from the supermarket; kids sauntering home from school; an elderly man leaving Ladbrokes on the Ewell Road, tucking the paper under his arm before walking home."

Everyday life must have felt a long way away after a once-in-a-lifetime bet on a horse who "seemed to gallop in another dimension."

GOLD SEAM (NEWMARKET) – AUGUST 26, 1989

Mark Coton's devotion to Major Dick Hern and Willie Carson had started long before Nashwan. "I followed them like other people followed football teams," he says, and a couple of months after Nashwan's spectacular Derby win, the combination of Hern, Carson and Pricewise struck gold once again.

Coton's August 26 column jostled for space on page seven with a report on the Ebor meeting in which Chief Inspector Jim Boam praised York racegoers as "a good, solid and very well-behaved crowd." Just one arrest was made during the three days although trans-Pennine relations weren't improved by the fact that "four off-duty Lancashire policemen" were arrested near the racecourse on the Tuesday.

Pricewise's focus was down south, however. Gold Seam was available at a general 7-2 for the *Mail On Sunday* Three Year Old Series Handicap at Newmarket. One firm, PM, were offering 4-1 about the favourite but Coton was certain that the Major's "good-looking three-year-old" would be popular with punters.

Mark Coton's favourite trainer-jockey combination: Major Dick Hern (left) and the grinning Willie Carson

"Such is the regard in which Gold Seam is held that the starting price could easily be around the 7-4 mark," he wrote. "He struck winning form in no uncertain style at Leicester last time and rates sparkling value at the 7-2 offered by Coomes, Dennis and Eden. Gold Seam was heavily backed before the Leicester race and won in great style [...] today's longer trip of seven furlongs should prove ideal and Hern is in super form, improving his excellent Newmarket record yesterday with the impressive Marienski."

Coton's disdain for blinkered form obsessives was thinly veiled in the next sentence of his preview. "Form book students will point out that Gold Seam looks to have plenty to do with top weight," he wrote, "but he has plenty of scope and must not be missed at the 7-2." As Pricewise predicted, the market had the utmost confidence in Willie Carson's mount, who was backed in to 2-1 by the off, and comfortably beat Bollin Zola despite conceding 19lb to the runner-up.

Gold Seam went on to win the Kiveton Park Stakes at Doncaster in September before an unsuccessful tilt at the Prix de la Forêt. Timeform reported that the horse's "rise from relative obscurity in the second half of the season was really quite meteoric." Along with the comet-like Nashwan, Gold Seam ensured that Coton's loyalty to his favourite trainer-jockey combination had paid off handsomely for Pricewise followers.

MULTUM IN PARVO (CHELTENHAM) – NOVEMBER 10, 1990

The Mackeson Gold Cup had provided a significant winner for Mark Coton's Pricewise, when Beau Ranger won the Cheltenham handicap in November 1987. Three years later the same race helped Mel Collier stake his claim to become Coton's full-time successor.

"After Mark stopped doing Pricewise there was a strange period when three or four of the tipsters would take it in turns to do the column," Collier recalls. "It wasn't the most important tipping piece in the paper at the time – that was still considered to be Diomed – and there was some scrimmaging about who should take it on full time or if it should even be a one-man job at all.

"I remember getting called into the editor's office one Friday and basically being told that the standard of my tips and analysis wasn't quite up to scratch and they would look elsewhere. I'd even gone and tipped some ridiculous thing in the Mackeson the next day that hadn't even had a pipe-opener that season. How was it going to win off a seven-month break?"

The "ridiculous thing" in question was Multum In Parvo, which was available at 14-1 in the morning. Collier already had an ante-post tip running for him in the race, as he reminded readers in his introduction: "Pricewise followers who took our advice to back Captain Mor each way in the Mackeson at 12-1 on Tuesday will be feeling pretty smug now. Arthur Stephenson's gelding is now best-priced at 13-2 with Stanley and his shortening highlights yet again the tremendous ante-post value to be had in these big Saturday jumps handicaps."

The Saturday column appeared above a bizarre advertisement offering *Racing Post* readers a video entitled 'Beginner's Guide To Tic-Tac'. The ad featured an illustration of a seedy-looking man in a flat cap and bow tie demonstrating the "top of the head" sign. "Easily learnt," it promised. "Discover the secrets. Gain the advantage. Amaze your friends. Profit from the knowledge."

The really profitable knowledge could be found higher up the page, however, in Collier's preview. Pinpointing the dangers to Captain Mor, he tipped Multum In Parvo, who "ran a tremendous race over course and distance at the Festival when a short-head second to Brown Windsor." The race could pan out to his liking, Collier predicted, as "with four or five confirmed front-runners in the field, his jockey will be given an ideal opportunity to cover him up then pounce with a late run."

Pricewise readers were also pointed in the direction of another value alternative, Thar-An-Bharr. "Significantly short with Ladbrokes and the Tote, he will attract plenty of each-way money at 20-1," Collier wrote. As it turned out, his analysis of both the market and the race was immaculate.

Thar-An-Bharr had halved in price by the start of the race and finished second, eight lengths behind Multum In Parvo, whose jockey Norman Williamson appeared to have read the Pricewise script. Held up early on, he took the lead approaching the last and ran on strongly. "I started doing the job full time soon after," Collier says wryly.

PASTERNAK (NEWMARKET) – OCTOBER 4, 1997

For some people, the name Pasternak evokes images of vast Russian steppes, smuggled manuscripts and Julie Christie wrapped up in furs. Racing fans, however, will be reminded of a huge gamble on the 1997 Cambridgeshire in which Pricewise, perhaps inevitably, played a part.

The non-literary Pasternak was trained by Sir Mark Prescott and owned by a syndicate whose members included Graham Rock, the *Racing Post*'s founding editor. Rock's fondness for a bet was legendary, and Mel Collier was spot on in Saturday's Pricewise when he described Pasternak as "the potential steamer" of the race.

"He has been very quiet in the ante-post market because of doubts about his participation," Collier wrote. "But now that he looks set to run he is sure to attract plenty of interest. Glancing down the runners, he is the one horse in the race who could still be thrown in. You just do not know how good he is [...] probably a lot better than the bare form suggests."

Pasternak, who landed a massive gamble in the Cambridgeshire in 1997, with owner Graham Rock

Pasternak (2pts win at 11-1) was actually Collier's second tip in the Cambridgeshire, with 33-1 shot Silk St John, who finished 12th, topping the bill. The *Racing Post* as a whole, though, only had eyes for one horse. The paper's unambiguous – and unprecedented – front-page headline was "Why you must back Pasternak."

Collier had predicted that the horse "could start around the 6-1 mark" but even that underestimated the scale of the coup. Rock, in an *Observer* article published posthumously in November 2001, wrote that "the public loved Pasternak, and the *Racing Post* fuelled the flames with its Saturday headline. Twenty-four hours before the big race he was on offer at 12-1, but at the off had been backed down to 4-1, one of the biggest gambles of recent times."

If the public had loved Pasternak before the Cambridgeshire then by the end of the race they were delirious about him. Sent off as 4-1 favourite – in a field of 36 – he was prominent throughout under George Duffield, hitting the front inside the final furlong and holding on by three-quarters of a length from Rudimental, also trained by Sir Mark Prescott.

A dazed Rock collected the trophy before filing his report to *The Observer*. "Words are wonderful," it began "but the variety of language is sometimes inadequate to convey an emotion so pure that only personal experience can suffice. Pasternak, carrying the colours of your racing correspondent, landed a major public gamble when winning the Tote Cambridgeshire from his stable companion Rudimental."

Four years later, Rock described his triumphant drive home after Pasternak's victory. In a vignette that demonstrates the emotive power of racing and betting, he wrote that "the sun was inching towards the horizon. We cruised through the flat East Anglian landscape, fields and trees brushed with scarlet and gold. The magic of the moment flashed before my eyes every few minutes. I remember thinking that I could die a happy man."

It was appropriate that the *Racing Post* – and Pricewise in particular – should have given the Pasternak gamble momentum. As editor, Rock had authorised the launch of the Pricewise column. His punting instincts had been aroused by Mark Coton's idea and his approval paved the way for hundreds of subsequent winners. Few, however, would be more spectacular than Pasternak.

TURNPOLE (NEWMARKET) – OCTOBER 18, 1997

Just two weeks after Pasternak's costly Cambridgeshire win, bookmakers must have been hoping for some respite. Collier, however, was in merciless form. The Cesarewitch was his kind of race, he wrote, because "a lot of the market leaders looked good on their midsummer, fast-ground form a few weeks ago but suddenly look vulnerable on softish ground and/or at the end of a hard season."

This criteria eliminated the likes of Mawared, Canon Can and Media Star ("another badly-priced animal") but "the one to be on is Turnpole at 28-1 with Sunderlands, who are not only top price, but offer a quarter the odds the first five."

"I was always on the lookout for a 'code switcher'," Collier says. "A good flat horse who had got in lightly when sent handicap hurdling or the other way round – a solid jumps horse who could take advantage of a lowly mark on the flat. They'd often be great value in one of the big staying flat handicaps like the Chester Cup, the Ascot Stakes, or in Turnpole's case, the Cesarewitch.

"Steve Mason gave Turnpole a *Racing Post* Rating of 139 over hurdles yet he came into the Ces off a flat rating of 74, despite finishing first or second in four of his five subsequent runs on the flat. Sometimes it really is that simple. Thinking about that tip makes me nostalgic for the days when 74-rated horses made the line-up in big handicaps!"

Turnpole, tipped by Mel Collier at 28-1, wins the Cesarewitch in 1997

Turnpole's lowly rating may not have impressed the bookmakers but Collier argued that punters should not be so dismissive. "Mary Reveley does well in the Cesarewitch with lightly-weighted horses," he wrote. "She has saddled a third (rated 79) and a winner (rated 66) in the last four years and Turnpole (rated 74 and racing bang on the minimum weight of 7st 10lb) looks a similar type."

There were no concerns over the horse's stamina – it had won over two-and-a-half miles over the jumps and, Collier predicted, "will relish the give in the ground and is a tough, consistent type." Reveley's charge – backed in to 16-1 – took up the running with more than three furlongs to go and never looked like being caught. In second was the 5-1 favourite Top Cees, who was described in the Pricewise preview as the only short-priced horse to fear.

Turnpole raced on for several more seasons, returning to Newmarket – without success – for the Cesarewitch in 2000 and winning as a ten-year-old at Pontefract in September 2001. "I remember the Tote odds compiler saying that he personally fancied the horse," Collier says. "The firm had taken next to nothing for it ante-post, though, so he stuck his neck out and went 25-1, hoping to attract a bit of money. He got more than he bargained for and the horse went from being a big winner to their worst loser! It almost made me feel sorry for them. Almost."

COOL DAWN (CHELTENHAM) – MARCH 19, 1998

Pricewise followers were still enjoying the warm glow of Pasternak and Turnpole's glorious autumn double when Collier turned his attention to the Cheltenham Festival. His ante-post Gold Cup feature was spread over three pages in the January 13, 1998 edition of the *Racing Post* and included profiles of 20 leading contenders, along with quotes from their connections.

Sally Alner, the wife of Cool Dawn's trainer Robert, gave an endearingly frank assessment of their plans for the horse: "He'll be entered for races at Ascot and Haydock at the end of this month and for the *Racing Post* Chase, but we are making it up as we go along." Collier seemed to approve of this carefree attitude and, more by a process of elimination than anything else, he came up with a headline tip of Cool Dawn, a 33-1 shot for the Gold Cup.

"He was a solid third in the Irish National in April 1996," Collier wrote, "and he impressed when a decisive winner of the Betterware Cup [at Ascot] last month." However, Cool Dawn's form was merely a detail – it was his enormous potential that made him a value bet. Collier conceded that the Alner runner was "unproven in the top class" but stressed that he "is on the upgrade."

The Pricewise "conclusion" began with a wise piece of advice. "As an ante-post punter, it pays to have a brutal analytical style to weed out the bad value," wrote Collier. "So it's goodbye to Dorans Pride (poor last run, not proven at the trip), Imperial Call (still to prove he retains all his old ability) and The Grey Monk (a flat-track bully who finds little in a finish) at single-figure prices." As Tom Segal discussed in Chapter Five, that ruthless streak is particularly useful at Cheltenham, where sentimentality and tribalism can affect even the most hard-hearted bettor. Segal ignored the hype surrounding Long Run and Kauto Star in the 2012 Gold Cup and, as a result, landed a 14-1 winner.

Collier's red pen continued its rampage through the list of Gold Cup entries. He swiftly eliminated "old boys" Rough Quest and Barton Bank on the grounds of age; Strong Promise, Challenger de Luc and Simply

Dashing were cast aside because of stamina concerns; while "a lot of the others are on the downgrade or unproven after injury troubles." The doubts over so many of the leading players seemed to support trainer David Nicholson's opinion about the race. Asked about possible runner Escartefigue, Nicholson said: "I've entered him because, despite what anyone else might think, I reckon the Gold Cup is wide open this year and we want to keep our options open."

It was a good race for Pricewise to tackle, then, and Collier was in no doubt about which horse he wanted on his side. "The best value is Cool Dawn at 33-1," he declared, recommending an eight-point win bet. "There is plenty of scope for his price to contract between now and March if he continues to show improved form in top-class handicaps [...] Postmark rates him around a stone behind Gold Cup class at the moment, but I would rather be on an improver with the scope to bridge the gap than horses such as Danoli, Nahthen Lad or Coome Hill who have all looked Gold Cup material at one time or another, but whose form has flattened out."

Cool Dawn's route to the Cheltenham Festival was a reminder of the stresses and strains faced by ante-post punters. Ten days after the Pricewise Gold Cup feature, he beat three rivals at Ascot after being sent off a 10-11 favourite. Despite a blunder at the second fence, he ran on well to score by two lengths from Orswell Lad. On February 7, he was once again favourite, at 5-4, in a six-runner handicap at Sandown but was pulled up by Andrew Thornton with three fences left to jump. Robert Alner told the stewards that the gelding had trapped a nerve in its shoulder. That setback meant that Cool Dawn's price did not contract to the extent that Collier had anticipated and he was still available at 25-1 on Gold Cup day.

At the seventh fence, Cyborgo was pulled up and Indian Tracker and See More Business – Collier's second ante-post selection at 12-1, sent off an 11-2 second-favourite – were carried out but Cool Dawn was blissfully unaware of the trouble in behind. Having made all the running, he stayed on stoutly to win by just under two lengths from Strong Promise with the 9-4 favourite Dorans Pride (a 7-1 chance when Collier wrote his ante-post preview) in third.

The video of Cool Dawn's Gold Cup is available on YouTube, where one viewer commented that "the noise in the background is the sound of a thousand form books being thrown through windows." The result didn't come as a shock to Pricewise followers, though, thanks to Mel Collier's unerring eye for a potential star.

PAPILLON (AINTREE) – APRIL 8, 2000

Papillon may not have been tipped up on the *Racing Post*'s front page like Pasternak but the paper certainly didn't conceal its enthusiasm for Ted Walsh's Grand National challenger. "The whole office was buzzing about him on the Friday," Collier recalls. "I've always tried to listen to as many points of view about a race as possible so I would often ask around to see what everyone fancied. For a supposed 33-1 rag, Papillon's name seemed to be popping up an awful lot. Colleagues Mel Cullinan, and a little-known Spotlight writer named Tom something – ah yes, Tom Segal – urged me to revisit my worries about the horse's stamina and, fortunately, I settled on the right one in the end."

"Papillon at 33-1 makes sense" was the Pricewise headline while, on

There was no false modesty from the Racing Post after Papillon landed what David Ashforth called "the biggest Grand National gamble in modern time" in April 2000.

the same page, Cullinan's Mark Your Card column declared: "Irish raider value to make big impression." Segal completed the hat-trick in the Spotlight verdict on the big race, writing that "conditions could well be ideal [for Papillon]; jumps and stays and is capable of winning if he puts it all in." The *Post's* Irish correspondent Tony O'Hehir also advised backing Walsh's runner.

Collier admitted in his preview that "there is not a great deal of encouragement to be found just looking at [Papillon's] recent form figures." Like Segal, though, he had been taken by the horse's performance in the 1998 Irish National, "a brave half-length second to last year's Aintree hero Bobbyjo."

The fact that three of the *Post's* most respected tipsters had identified the same 33-1 shot meant an inevitable plunge on Papillon but the scale of the gamble took Collier by surprise. "The hype got ramped up a bit more when Ted Walsh gave a bullish interview on 'The Morning Line' on the Saturday," he says. "From then on, punters just kept piling on and he was 10-1 second favourite at the off."

The trainer's bullishness wasn't misplaced as Papillon, under a 20-year-old Ruby Walsh, led home a 40-strong field, holding off Mely Moss by just over a length. While the Walsh family celebrated, bookmakers' hearts were in their boots. David Ashforth, writing in Monday's *Racing Post*, described it as "the biggest Grand National gamble in modern times" and Coral's Simon Clare said, "Suddenly, the day before the race, there was a buzz for it – a professional gamble, then a public gamble. Pricewise tipped it and, on normal racedays, Pricewise is the biggest single influence on the market."

The front-page headline of Monday's *Racing Post* asked: "Was it something we said? Papillon lands amazing multi-million-pound gamble sparked by *Post* tipsters." According to the news story, "punters across Britain and Ireland joined a raceday rush to back the Ted Walsh-trained gelding, prompted in many cases by the strong recommendations of Pricewise and three other *Racing Post* tipsters in Saturday's paper."

Collier took great pleasure in delivering the big-race winner. "The Grand National was the race that got me interested in racing in the first place," he says. "To be involved in one of the biggest winning gambles in the biggest race of the year was fantastic. And just to round off a perfect race, Papillon beat *The Sporting Life* tip into second place!"

HEIDI & INN AT THE TOP (DONCASTER) – JANUARY 27, 2001

Betting on racing can be a stressful business at times but Pricewise followers didn't have a moment's worry in the Great Yorkshire Chase of 2001 as the two horses tipped by Mel Collier jumped the last together, with 33-1 shot Heidi staying on best to beat Inn At The Top, advised at 11-1.

Monday's *Racing Post* carried a front-page picture of the Pricewise pair soaring over the final fence, beneath the headline "Tipping doesn't get any better than this." Understandably, Collier remembers the race well, describing it as "the proudest moment of my Pricewise stint. My tips finished first and second, 16 lengths clear of the horse in third. From quite a way out it was obvious that one or other was going to win – it was a dream position to be in, even before in-running betting was available."

Inn At The Top had been the headline selection, having won four of his five races at Doncaster. Collier outlined the factors in his favour: "He is game, has plenty of solid form in classy handicaps like this and – encouragingly – Jim Turner's small yard turned out a winner with its last runner four days ago."

Heidi was introduced to the readers as something of an inspired afterthought. "There is no value in the place book, which only pays out on the first three in this 15-runner race," Collier wrote. "Rather than backing [Inn At The Top] each-way, have another win bet on 33-1 shot Heidi. After winning over fences in France, he won three of his five hurdles starts in Britain and went into the notebook as one to follow over fences [...] trainer Micky Hammond reckons the horse has been 'crying out' for this three-mile trip."

With the rest of the field strung out behind them, Heidi's stamina proved decisive as jockey Dean Gallagher ground down Inn At The Top. The winner, tipped at 33-1, returned an SP of 20-1. "It was particularly pleasing that they finished in the 'right' order," says Collier. "The biggest-priced horse won and it was also nice that Heidi had been top price in the morning with Ladbrokes, who the conspiracy theorists often accused me of colluding with. It was always nice to tip a 'biggie' with the Magic Sign."

The *Racing Post*'s follow-up story hailed "the wonder of Pricewise" and "Melvyn Collier's astonishing run of big-priced winners." Remarkably, it was Collier's second spectacular 1-2 within a couple of months. "As regular followers will know, this was no flash in the pan," the *Post* reported. "In November, in almost a dress rehearsal for events on Saturday, Pricewise advised two horses for the Hennessy Cognac Gold Cup at Newbury with his 10-1 shot King's Road (2pts win) beating his 40-1 offering Gingembre (2pts win, 1pt place).

"This truly is the column the bookies fear," the piece concluded. And in the Great Yorkshire Chase the layers knew their fate earlier than usual.

MARSAD (NEWMARKET) – MAY 4, 2002

Tom Segal had taken over the Pricewise job permanently in the summer of 2001. By the start of the 2002 flat season, his tips were already making a serious impression on the market, as demonstrated by the John Akehurst-trained Marsad on 2,000 Guineas day at Newmarket.

The headline for the Pricewise column left readers in no doubt about the gelding's chances – "Marsad a 22-1 money-maker" – and Segal's introduction was also unequivocal. "Let's keep it simple when looking for the best bet of the day," he wrote. "The 30-runner ladbrokes.com Handicap (3.15) looks impossible at first glance, but last year's easy winner Marsad makes plenty of appeal this morning."

Marsad had won the race cosily in 2001, despite being slowly away, and the 22-1 about him retaining his crown was too big to ignore. Always on the lookout for a horse that had been targeted at a particular race, Segal believed that Akehurst's sprinter was set for a peak performance. "He has been aimed at a repeat performance for ages and really caught the eye when in need of the run over seven furlongs at Kempton on his reappearance," he wrote. "That will have brought him to a peak today and the word is that he's coming into this race in tip-top shape, better than when a close sixth in the vastly more competitive Ayr Gold Cup last season."

The gamble was fuelled by an encouraging quote from the trainer, who confirmed that "he has been trained for this and has come on for his Kempton run. My horses are running into form and, although he's 5lb higher than last year, I'm very hopeful." Another *Racing Post* tipster, Nick Fox of Betting Bureau, also identified Marsad as great value at 22-1, and punters concurred. Marsad opened up at 10-1 on-course and was smashed in to 11-2 joint-favouritism before hitting the front inside the final furlong and holding off 33-1 shot Peruvian Chief by a short head.

Although 30-runner handicaps weren't to Mark Coton's taste, he would have approved of the 'objective value' of a horse being tipped at 22-1 and going off at 11-2. Segal didn't enjoy a perfect afternoon – his advice in the 2,000 Guineas was "just sit back and watch Hawk Wing hack up" (the 6-4 favourite was narrowly beaten by stablemate Rock of Gibraltar) – but there was no quibbling with his reckoning that "everything really does look spot-on for Marsad today."

MONTY'S PASS (AINTREE) – APRIL 5, 2003

As a Spotlight writer in 2000, Segal had helped spark the public gamble on Papillon and his first Grand National winner as Pricewise was another "underrated Irish challenger." His ante-post National preview on February 5, 2003 began by advising punters to reassess the nature of the Aintree showpiece.

"The National is a changing race," Segal wrote, "and it can only be a

This headline proved to be spot on as Tom Segal's ante-post selection for the Grand National hosed up by 12 lengths under Barry Geraghty in 2003.

matter of time before the trends followers have to revise their thinking on the race because the handicapper has given those at the top of the handicap an outstanding chance of winning. Last year's race pointed at things to come, with many of those at the top of the handicap running big races. Provided the ground isn't bottomless, as it was in Red Marauder or Earth Summit's years, then the better, classy horses should by no means be discounted."

As usual with the Grand National, most of the market leaders were well known to punters and bookmakers. However, Segal reckoned there was more to come from Monty's Pass, who he had tipped the previous year when finishing second in the Topham Chase at Aintree. "I've a strong feeling that he has been crying out for the step up to extended trips and he has been given the winter off with this race in mind," he wrote. "Last year he ran a cracker in the Mildmay of Flete when a staying-on fifth and he subsequently jumped really well when runner-up over Aintree's big fences in the Topham Chase." Because Monty's Pass was a consistent, versatile type, he would give ante-post punters fewer worries than most of his rivals. "The other bonuses are that he jumps really well, goes on any ground and may well be ridden by crack Irish jockey Barry Geraghty," Segal concluded.

Geraghty did indeed take the ride, fresh from an outstanding Cheltenham Festival, and Monty's Pass did the rest, jumping fluently to win by 12 lengths from Supreme Glory. Bookmakers reported that the 16-1 shot was a good result for them on the day although Pricewise, and the winning owner Mike Futter, had caused them plenty of grief ante-post.

The *Racing Post* described Futter's coup as "a gamble of proportions unparalleled in Grand National history" but the Northern Ireland-based bingo magnate took it all in his stride. "It worked out exactly as we thought it would," he said. "A plan well executed, it worked to perfection and the dream came true."

Asked about the evolution of the gamble, the owner explained: "I started backing him at 66-1 before the weights came out. Then I backed him at 50-1, but then he was tipped in the *Racing Post* and the price started to come down. The biggest bet I had was £10,000 at 50-1." Futter estimated that his total winnings on the race (excluding prize money) was "in excess of £800,000." For once, Pricewise wasn't the bookmakers' biggest headache.

Attache wins the Buckingham Palace Handicap at Royal Ascot in 2003, completing a hat-trick for Pricewise

IN TIME'S EYE, SHANTY STAR & ATTACHE (ASCOT) – JUNE 20, 2003

Bookies are not noted for their love of Shakespeare but the Friday of Royal Ascot in 2003 may have prompted one or two layers to recall the line "when sorrows come, they come not single spies but in battalions." It was already looking like a good day for punters after victories for 5-2 favourite High Accolade and Russian Rhythm, who was backed in to 4-7 from 4-5. And then Tom Segal got to work.

In a *Racing Post* interview in 2007, Segal chose that golden Friday as the highlight of his tipping career. "Rather than pick out one race, I'm going to nominate about an hour and a half on the Friday of Royal Ascot 2003 as one of my defining days in the Pricewise hot seat," he wrote. "Big meetings are what it is all about, whether you're a trainer, jockey, owner, punter or tipster, so to suggest backing the last three winners at prices of 16-1, 6-1 and 33-1 was a huge thrill. The last winner, Attache, was particularly pleasing, because the consensus among experts had been that the near-side rail was hugely favoured. I took the opposite view, and Philip Robinson streaked up the far side to win narrowly at a starting price of just 10-1."

The prices about the previous two Pricewise selections had also collapsed. Dermot Weld's In Time's Eye – tipped at 16-1 for the Wolferton Handicap in the morning – was backed in to 5-1 while Shanty Star, from the in-form Mark Johnston stable, went off as 7-2 favourite for the Queen's Vase, having been 6-1 with Paddy Power.

Segal is always happy to trust the judgement of top trainers at the big meetings. Johnston, he wrote, "can add to his four winners this week in the Queen's Vase with Shanty Star, whom he regards as one of his best bets of the week." Likewise, "Dermot Weld is nobody's fool and the fact that he ran [In Time's Eye] in the Irish Derby last season and the Group 1 Tattersalls Gold Cup on his reappearance suggests that he has shown tons of ability at home."

As usual, Segal reasoned that the impact of the draw had been exaggerated, leading to some juicy prices in the final race on the card. "The bookmakers have priced the Buckingham Palace Handicap as if there were a massive low-draw bias, so there are some big prices floating about," he wrote. The biggest of these prices was the 33-1 about "the class horse Attache" who "beat a top-class field at Newmarket earlier in the season and loves fast ground and seven furlongs."

In Time's Eye landed the gamble by a narrow margin, holding off John Dunlop's Persian Lightning by a neck, before Shanty Star stayed on strongly to take the Queen's Vase by three-quarters of a length. The bookies were wobbling and Attache was primed to deliver the knockout punch. Sent off a 10-1 third-favourite, jockey Philip Robinson tracked the leaders on the unfancied far side, hitting the front with a furlong to go and winning by half a length from Hurricane Floyd.

Pricewise had delivered the winners of the last three races – the 4.20, the 4.55 and the 5.30 – racking up 86 points profit in the process. Simon Clare of Coral described the Friday as "a shocking day for Coral and In Time's Eye was the major factor." Ladbrokes pinned the blame on Attache who "turned a bad week into an atrocious week" according to the firm's spokesman

Balthazar Fabricius. Dale Tempest of Skybet, who had been top price about both In Time's Eye and Attache, called it "a disastrous day for us."

The *Racing Post* revelled in the flurry of winners. "Post men's barrage means carnage for layers" was the headline on page two of Saturday's edition. "Bookmakers were reeling last night after the *Racing Post*'s elite team of tipsters sparked an unforgettable day for punters at Royal Ascot," the story began. "The damage was chiefly inflicted by Pricewise (Tom Segal) and Trading Bureau (Nick Fox) in unearthing 33-1 chance Attache, who was backed down to 10-1 before winning the Buckingham Palace Handicap. "That followed wins for In Time's Eye (16-1 to 5-1 – tipped by Pricewise, Gerald Delamere and Tony O'Hehir) and Shanty Star (6-1 to 7-2 – tipped by Pricewise, Gerald Delamere and The North)." There really was no escape for the bookies.

MANA D'ARGENT (ASCOT) & FAR LANE (YORK) – JULY 12, 2003.

Such was Pricewise's hot streak in the summer of 2003 that, according to the *Racing Post*, bookmakers were "breathing a sigh of relief" because Segal had tipped 'only' two winners on the second Saturday of July. "Can Pricewise extend this super sequence?" asked the *Post*'s front-page headline, quoting not only Attache and In Time's Eye but also Fantastic Light (12-1), Orientor (10-1), Patavellian (9-1 in to 4-1) and Move It (7-1), all of whom had won in the last four weeks.

The answer came, initially, in the form of Mana D'Argent. Segal's case for Mark Johnston's stayer was based on the fact that it would be annoying if punters didn't back him and he won. "Given that Mana D'Argent is a much better horse at Ascot than elsewhere, if he wins the Tote Exacta Handicap at the Berkshire course, backers will kick themselves for not supporting him," he wrote. "So for comfort purposes we should have a small bet at 7-1."

That small bet was even more comforting by around 2.40pm, by which time Mana D'Argent had justified 5-1 favouritism, overhauling Thewhirlingdervish with 150 yards of the two miles remaining. He would finish his career with six wins, all of them at Ascot.

The "massively talented" Far Lane was a more confident selection for the John Smith's Cup at York. "This horse has been knocking on the door in many of the big handicaps since about this time last season and has been unlucky not to win at least two," Segal wrote. "But, for the first time, the four-year-old looks to have everything in his favour and, at 9-1 with Ladbrokes, he is the one to be on."

Far Lane's "tactical speed" could be crucial, Segal argued, particularly as he "should enjoy the run of the race from stall four." The Barry Hills runner "was unlucky not to win the Cambridgeshire and the Autumn Cup at Newbury last year and is rated a better horse this season by connections. He can finally win the big one he deserves." It was indeed Far Lane's day. Despite hanging left in the final furlong, the four-year-old saw off David Loder's Etesaal by half a length, landing a 47-1 SP coup for any Pricewise followers who put him in a double with Mana D'Argent.

Bookmakers were fearing the worst when Segal's tip in the next race at York – Spanish John in the Webster's Silver Cup – was backed from 16-1 in to 9-2. The top-weight raced prominently for much of the 1m 6f before fading into sixth, saving the layers from a monster payout. "It's a tribute to Tom Segal that Spanish John should go off at just 9-2, due to the liabilities," said Victor Chandler spokesman Neal Wilkins. "If he had won, it would have been as bad a day as the Friday of Royal Ascot." Coral's David Stevens added, "There is no doubt that two big winners in televised races on a Saturday would have cost several millions across the industry – if Spanish John had won as well you could probably multiply that a few times."

For Blue Square, it was the end of a particularly painful week at the hands of Pricewise, as the firm's spokesman Ed Pownall explained. "On Thursday we were standout about Patavellian and there were a lot of new accounts opened," Pownall said. "They were full of money and they kept following [Segal] for the rest of the week. I was pleasantly surprised that we were just six figures down. If Spanish John had won it would have been an absolute nightmare."

LAFI & FAYR JAG (ASCOT) – JUNE 19, 2004

Like Mana D'Argent, Segal seemed to raise his game at Ascot and on the Saturday of the 2004 Royal Ascot meeting he was responsible for what Coral describe as one of their worst day's racing ever. The firm were top price in the morning about both Pricewise winners: Fayr Jag in the Golden Jubilee and Lafi in the Wokingham.

Lafi wins the Wokingham in 2004, under Eddie Ahern, giving Tom Segal a double on the day

Fayr Jag had dead-heated with Ratio in the Wokingham in 2003 – a performance which, Segal believed, made him a major player in the Golden Jubilee. "Last year's Wokingham was such a strong race that Fayr Jag must have a good chance if he can repeat that level of form," he wrote. "That day he had the likes of The Tatling and Patavellian behind, and when he went on to win in Group company in Ireland under similar conditions he easily beat today's favourite Avonbridge, despite suffering trouble in running.

"The slight misgiving I have about his chance is his draw in stall nine, because most of the fancied horses are drawn nearer the rail, but they are bound to go off at a million miles an hour and if the ground remains fast Fayr Jag has a sound chance of winning at the top level. The 16-1 with Coral looks well worth taking."

Tim Easterby's five-year-old was nibbled at in the betting, going off at 12-1 with Avonbridge a 100-30 favourite. Driven out by Willie Supple, Fayr Jag pipped Crystal Castle by a head with Cape Of Good Hope a further head back in third. The first three finishers had all been held up, underlining Segal's theory that patience is the primary virtue for jockeys in big sprints.

Pricewise sided with another sprinter from Easterby's yard in the Wokingham, tipping Dazzling Bay, who would finish fifth, at a general 12-1. However, Segal was also keen on the 9-1 morning favourite. "Lafi must also be backed from stall 30, having really caught the eye at Epsom last time when considered not quite at his peak," he wrote. "That will have put him spot-on for today and he has some classy form to his name, having thrashed a good field under a big weight at Sandown last season. If he had run well at this track before I would be very confident, but he has tons of speed and the plum draw, so the 9-1 with Coral is more than fair. The fact that he stays seven furlongs is a big plus too, because this is a stiff track and those who have proved themselves over that bit further have a good record in the race."

Lafi, backed in to 6-1 favouritism, showed all his class and stamina, storming home by a length and a half from Coconut Penang. The combination of an in-form Segal, a couple of sprint handicaps and Royal Ascot added up to trouble for bookmakers – and double trouble for Coral.

SERGEANT CECIL (NEWCASTLE) – JUNE 25, 2005

Few flat horses have inspired such affection in recent years as Sergeant Cecil and Rod Millman's stayer holds a special place in Tom Segal's heart. The Sergeant's win in the Northumberland Plate heralded the start of Pricewise's ten straight winning Saturdays during the summer of 2005 and Segal remains grateful.

He told the *Racing Post* in 2007 that "a lot of the credit for that run must go to one horse in particular, Sergeant Cecil. He started the run by winning the Northumberland Plate at the end of June and it was his success that proved to me that the harder you study a race, the more complicated it becomes and the more horses you end up fancying."

Segal demonstrated his fondness for Irish racing by leading Saturday's Pricewise column on the chances of well-travelled filly Alexander Goldrun in the Pretty Polly Stakes at The Curragh. "In Hong Kong last season, she beat Bullish Luck in a Group 1 that also included the likes of Rakti," he wrote. "Don't forget that Bullish Luck recently got the better of the superstar Silent Witness [...] Basically, she has done it and got the T-shirt, while her rivals still have it all to prove." Pricewise advised a two-point bet at 9-2 on Alexander Goldrun, who went off the 9-4 favourite and won comfortably.

However, the column's headline focused on the Northumberland Plate – "20-1 Sergeant Cecil set to dispel any stamina doubts" – and Segal was confident that the step up to two miles wouldn't be beyond his selection. "Provided the ground stays on the quick side at Newcastle, it could be worth chancing the stamina of Sergeant Cecil at a huge price," he began. "This is a top-quality handicapper" who "never runs a bad race when the ground is on the lively side. The trip is a slight worry but in some of the best mile-and-three-quarter handicaps last year he was staying on best of all late on and it could be that the step up to two miles sees him improve on what is already rock-solid form. In Alan Munro he has one of the better tactical jockeys" and "if the ground is quick he is certainly no 20-1 shot."

The Pitmen's Derby that year featured a couple of major market moves, independent of Pricewise. Far Pavilions had been all the rage in the ante-post betting and was 4-1 favourite in the morning, before drifting to 6-1. Swift Sailor – an early-priced 7-1 – was sent off the 7-2 favourite but could only finish mid-division, well behind Sergeant Cecil who, in the evocative words of the *Racing Post* analysis, "weaved through to lead inside final furlong, kept on strongly."

Everything had gone right for Segal's tip – the ground at Newcastle was good, Munro's tactics were spot on and Sergeant Cecil's stamina never looked like failing him. It was a sign of the glorious summer to come.

COURAGEOUS DUKE (HAYDOCK) – AUGUST 6, 2005

The five Saturdays after Sergeant Cecil and Alexander Goldrun produced six more winners for Pricewise. After Zeitgeist (14-1), Mullins Bay (5-1), Another Bottle (12-1), La Cucaracha (13-2), Azamour (11-4) and Gift Horse (5-1), the *Racing Post*'s front page on August 6, 2005 featured silhouetted horses galloping beneath apocalyptic skies and the headline "7th Heaven?" "Big-priced winners on six consecutive Saturdays – now the world's top tipping service goes for seven," the sub-deck explained. "Do you believe in the power of Pricewise?"

Page three carried ragouts of the previous six weeks' tips, along with a story by Lee Mottershead that started: "Titter ye not at their suffering. Rather pity the poor bookmakers, for suffering they are and poor they may soon be. Fillet steak has been replaced on dinner tables by corned beef. The Bolly has been traded in for orange squash. Even the pet budgies have had their seed rationed. And it's all down to that pesky Pricewise."

The man at the centre of the story was playing down the hype. "I don't feel the pressure of a winning run," Segal explained. "Each race is different and you can only try to tip the winner of that race. It is just a matter of looking ahead to the next race and not back at the last six weeks." While Segal refused to blow his own trumpet, bookmakers were grimly acknowledging his brilliance. William Hill's David Hood called Pricewise "a phenomenon" and Coral's Simon Clare said, "In the first hour [of business] two-thirds of all calls will be for the Pricewise horses."

Courageous Duke was the horse that epitomised the sense of inevitability about Pricewise tips that summer. As Segal told *The Guardian* in September 2005, "He hadn't won for two or three years and normally I don't like tipping horses like that. But the race had fallen apart for him; everything had come right and I was able to see that."

"The hardest thing to lose in racing is a reputation," Segal's preview began "but Courageous Duke can confound the critics who have him down as a nearly horse and a non-winner by landing the Totesport Handicap at Haydock this afternoon." He admitted that the horse wasn't "brilliantly handicapped" but "with the services of Kieren Fallon" and "the fast ground that he loves [...] it is really hard not to see him running a very big race."

It was a mark of the public confidence in Segal that Courageous Duke, whose last win had come 15 runs and 25 months ago, was sent off the 7-2 favourite, having been tipped at 8-1. Slowly away, he was held up by Fallon before tackling Eccentric in the final furlong and going on to win by three-quarters of a length.

Bookmakers' responses were beginning to sound a little tetchy. Balthazar Fabricius of Ladbrokes said: "It's becoming a bit repetitive now and it's not good news for us. It was another poor day for the bookies but I don't expect anyone to be shedding a tear for us." Coral were top price about Courageous Duke and Simon Clare admitted that "of all the seven

Saturdays where Pricewise has had a winner, that is by far the worst. We're waving the white flag now." And William Hill's Jennie Prest offered the greatest tribute that any bookie could pay to a tipster, describing Segal as "a damned nuisance." The layers would be calling him even worse names before the summer was out.

ASHKAL WAY (BEVERLEY) – AUGUST 20, 2005

A week after Courageous Duke came Ice Planet which, remarkably, drifted from 8-1 to 10-1 before slamming 22 rivals to claim the William Hill Great St Wilfrid Handicap at Ripon. Punters weren't going to make the same mistake again and Ashkal Way, who gave Pricewise a ninth successive winning Saturday, was backed as if defeat was out of the question.

The *Racing Post*'s front page featured a footballer with his back to the camera wearing a mocked-up 'Pricewise 9' shirt. "Bring on number nine," the headline cried, adding that "when Saturday comes, no striker's more prolific than Pricewise." Ordinarily, Segal might have been expected to focus on the card at his hometown track. However, as he explained, "with the ground likely to be desperate at best at Sandown this afternoon, the safest port of call for a bet in the early price races has to be at Beverley."

Ashkal Way was a standout 13-2 with Blue Square and that price made plenty of appeal. "Brian Ellison has his horses in cracking form," Segal wrote, "and the word is that Ashkal Way has been working very well in the run-up to today." His eye for an underrated jockey also came into play as he assured readers that "further confidence comes from the booking of crack Irish apprentice Chris Hayes, who has had seven winners already this month, including a hat-trick at Gowran Park a couple of weeks ago. I can hear you saying that that is all well and good, but what does he know of Beverley? Well, he rode a winner here for Ellison earlier in the year too." The apprentice received the Segal stamp of approval: "Having watched Hayes closely I would suggest that he is already as good as most of the jockeys he's up against today and his [5lb] claim is a gift."

With a trainer and jockey who were in almost as good form as Pricewise, the result was never in doubt. Ashkal Way was smashed off the boards and the 2-1 favourite cruised home by three lengths from Pieter Brueghel with third-placed River Falcon a further three lengths back.

On page three of Sunday's *Racing Post*, Paul Eacott wrote that "supporters of the phenomenal Pricewise tipping service were on cloud nine last night after finding themselves in the money for an incredible ninth consecutive Saturday." The notion of value, as Mark Coton would define it, was lost in the scramble to get on Segal's tips, however. Coral's Simon Clare sounded a little bemused about the cost to his firm of the Ashkal Way plunge. "It's been a shocking result for us, even though we ducked it," Clare said. "There is now such a huge Pricewise following that people will take the 5s even when it's 13-2 elsewhere."

The tenth and final nail in the bookmakers' coffins came on August 27 when, as described in Chapter Three, Tax Free landed a colossal gamble to win the William Hill Trophy at York. Like Olga Korbut at the 1972 Munich Olympics, Pricewise had completed a perfect ten.

STAR DE MOHAISON & NEWMILL (CHELTENHAM) – MARCH 15, 2006

Most punters would be happy enough to have a couple of 33-1 ante-post selections lining up at Cheltenham; on the Wednesday of the 2006 Festival, Pricewise followers were celebrating a pair of 33-1 winners.

The January 31 edition of the *Racing Post* carried Pricewise's ante-post feature on the Queen Mother Champion Chase. Segal's piece was accompanied by Craig Thake's trends analysis, which advised: "One fact stands out: don't go looking for longshots at this stage. Only one of the last ten winners was available at bigger than 10-1 at the end of January." Trends are there to be broken, however, and Segal believed that the 2006 Champion Chase was an open affair. "With Azertyuiop injured, Well Chief not entered and Moscow Flyer a light of his former self this season [it] doesn't look a strong renewal at this stage," he wrote.

The market was led by Kauto Star, a horse who would rewrite the Cheltenham history books over the next five years, but Segal was happy to oppose the favourite at the prices: "He may turn out to love quick ground and prove to be the superstar that many believe but 7-4 for the Champion Chase six weeks beforehand? No thanks."

Fota Island was "by far the most solid of those at the head of the market" and worth a bet at 7-1 but "at a much bigger price the one I am especially keen on is another Irish horse, Newmill." Segal's eye had been caught by a race that most English tipsters and punters might have missed. Newmill "was mightily impressive when switched back to fences at Thurles 12 days ago. The form of that two-and-a-half miler is not that strong but the time was impressive and anyone who saw the race will know that this is a horse of the highest class. He is a massive price at 33-1 given that there is very little strength in depth to this year's Champion Chase."

On February 14, Segal turned his attention to what he described as his favourite Festival race for ante-post purposes: the Royal & SunAlliance Novices' Chase. He was looking for a horse who would cope with a "real war of attrition" but who also had "the ability to jump cleanly at pace."

"I think the race has a really nice shape to it once again," Segal wrote, "because I just don't believe current favourite Darkness jumps anything like well enough to win. In fact, I think he'll have a job getting round, so bad was his last jumping effort at Sandown."

Our Ben – "who ran his best race over hurdles at the Festival a year ago and has been trained with the race in mind since" – was advised at 7-1 but Segal was more enthusiastic about an each-way bet on Paul Nicholls' Star De Mohaison at 33-1. "Twice beaten by The Listener on ground a bit soft this season, Star De Mohaison finished like a rocket when third to that horse at Cheltenham and would have beaten him over three miles," he wrote. "Quite how he is 33-1 and The Listener around 8-1, I'll never know."

Any readers who remained unconvinced by Star De Mohaison's potential would surely have been won over by Segal's closing remarks. "Quite simply," he concluded, "this horse jumps brilliantly, stays forever, has plenty of class and needs good ground – all the attributes required to win the SunAlliance." You didn't need to read between the lines to work out that this was a serious tip.

Neither Newmill nor Star De Mohaison raced again before Cheltenham but both lined up on March 15 at far shorter prices than those at which they'd been tipped by Pricewise. Star De Mohaison was 14-1 on the day but the Royal & SunAlliance got off to a bad start for Segal as Our Ben, his other tip, unseated Ruby Walsh at the third fence. 9-2 favourite Commercial Flyer was pulled up, The Listener – Star De Mohaison's old rival – was outpaced before falling two out, and poor jumping hampered the chances of Darkness, who finished a distant third. None of this concerned Barry Geraghty on Star De Mohaison, who was always prominent, took up the running four fences from home, and powered on to beat Idle Talk by six lengths. Segal had given the five-year-old a huge build-up and Star De Mohaison delivered a truly authoritative performance.

Around 40 minutes later, Pricewise's lightning again struck the same patch of Cotswold countryside. While the 2-1 favourite Kauto Star fell and Moscow Flyer struggled to make an impression on the race, eventually finishing fifth, 16-1 shot Newmill made all. Driven clear approaching the final fence, he gave his pursuers no chance, winning by nine lengths from Fota Island, who completed a 1-2 for Pricewise.

It was the ante-post equivalent of Segal's glorious Friday of Royal Ascot in 2003. Two 33-1 winners in the space of three-quarters of an hour – with a combined winning distance of 15 lengths – represented an extraordinary feat of tipping.

NUMBERSIXVALVERDE (AINTREE) – APRIL 8, 2006

The day after putting up Newmill for the Champion Chase, Segal had another high-profile ante-post assignment – the Grand National. "Up until a few years ago, I thought I had the Grand National taped," he wrote. "What you needed was a horse who had shown the ability to travel and jump well and had run well in one of the top staying races in the past. Sounds simple – and it was, with the likes of Bobbyjo and Papillon following the script perfectly." Now, however, "I don't really think there is an archetypal National horse."

This was a discouraging development for most punters but Segal reckoned there was still value to be had in the ante-post market. "I can see last year's winner Hedgehunter going very close again," he advised but the two contenders that stood out were Silver Birch at 16-1 and Numbersixvalverde, a nightmare for headline writers but an exciting bet at 25-1.

Numbersixvalverde "should run well, having caught the eye when staying on strongly over hurdles recently," Segal wrote. "He looks well weighted and stays very well, so I can't resist a few quid on him at 25-1. Hopefully it will be a real stamina test this year because that is what suits Numbersixvalverde best, and if that's the case, and his jumping holds up, not many, if any, will be staying on better than him."

Trainer Martin Brassil's charge warmed up for Aintree by finishing third over 2m 3f on heavy ground at Naas in March. He was far from dismissed by punters on Grand National day, starting as the 11-1 fifth favourite behind 5-1 market leaders Hedgehunter and Clan Royal. The joint-favourites looked to have it between them with five fences remaining before Numbersixvalverde crashed the party. His jockey, Niall 'Slippers' Madden, stayed out of trouble on the first circuit, slowly creeping into contention and tackling Hedgehunter as they jumped the last. Segal had predicted that few horses would be staying on better than Numbersixvalverde at the bitter end and he was proved right. The top-weight couldn't go with him and Madden, an Aintree rookie, drove his mount on to win by six lengths.

Pricewise's second tip had only been 12 months out – Silver Birch, who had been in contention until falling at The Chair in 2006, made amends by winning the 2007 Grand National with Numbersixvalverde, in his final race, back in sixth.

FURNACE & RELATIVE ORDER (ASCOT) – SEPTEMBER 27, 2008

Seeing the horse you've backed in a 29-runner handicap beaten a head is usually a thoroughly dispiriting experience. It wasn't so bad for Pricewise followers in the Totesport.com Challenge Cup at Ascot in 2008, however, as Tom Segal not only tipped the runner-up Relative Order but also the winner, Furnace, at 16-1.

The Ascot handicap was an example of Segal's theory that, however big the field, it can soon be whittled down to a handful of possible winners. He also advised readers not to waste their time trying to solve the riddle of the draw but instead to focus on the horses' ability and scope for improvement.

"It has to be said that the Ascot straight track is impossible to fathom," he wrote. "Winners, like kamikaze pilots, come from left, right and centre and nearly always when least expected but I do like the look of Furnace and Relative Order from high draws, both at a general 16-1. I have no clue whether high numbers will be at an advantage, and there is pace on both sides, but in these two we have in-form improvers against a mostly ageing and exposed bunch."

Both selections were still open to improvement, Segal believed. "Relative Order first caught my eye when staying on really strongly to win at the Shergar Cup meeting last year and since then has done nothing but improve," he wrote. "I'm certain he loves a stiff seven and coming late off a strong pace so everything looks right for him today.

The newspaper clipping reads:

Saturday, September 27, 2008 racingpost.co.uk

PRICEWISE

Relative value at 16-1 – and Furnace looks hot stuff too

THE Queen Elizabeth II Stakes is the mile race of the season, and of many seasons for that matter, and, despite the ground coming in Henrythenavigator's favour, I am firmly in the Tamayuz camp.

There is no obvious reason to believe he won't like fast ground – in fact, he could improve for it – and he is such an easy ride that I cannot see any scenario in the Sony-backed contest that won't suit him.

Having said that, he is not one to back this morning because I think he is going to drift as the big hitters get stuck into Henry, and it is the Tote-sponsored handicap (3.40) that catches my attention, as you may expect.

To start with, it has to be said the Ascot straight track is impossible to fathom, with winners, like kamikaze pilots, coming from left, right and centre and nearly always when least expected, but I do like the look of Furnace and Relative Order from high draws, both at a general 16-1.

I have no clue whether high numbers will be at an advantage, and there is pace on both sides, but in these two we have in-form improvers against a mostly ageing and exposed bunch.

Relative Order first caught my eye when staying on really strongly to win at the Shergar Cup meeting last year and since then has done nothing but improve. At Goodwood, in a good three-year-old handicap this year, he showed a great turn of foot to

Today's advice

Orizaba
2.30 Ascot
1pt win at 4-1 generally

Relative Order
3.40 Ascot
1pt win at 16-1 generally

Furnace
3.40 Ascot
1pt win at 16-1 generally

be third, and that was a very meritorious effort, considering he was drawn in stall 1. He followed that with a comfortable win over a decent yardstick at Newmarket.

Last time, Relative Order didn't enjoy the run of the race over a mile on sand but he still performed well and I'm certain he loves a stiff seven and coming late off a strong pace – so everything looks right for him today.

The Michael Bell-trained **Furnace**, despite being a year older, is less exposed and came right back to form when winning a competitive race at Chester last time from an outside draw.

Seldom do you see horses involved in the finish, let alone win, if they have raced wide on his racetrack run last time. That is what Furnace achieved, and the way he battled back after being headed suggested there was plenty left in the tank.

Furnace was ridden too prominently and didn't get home in the Britannia here last year, but he ran well all the same, which shows he can handle the track, and there is every chance he is still on the upgrade.

Of the others, good sand horse Atlantic Story is dangerous back at 7f, having shaped well over six at Doncaster on soft ground on his racetrack run last time. That should have put him spot-on and, from stall 26, he should get a good row from Tamagin.

The opening fillies' handicap is wide open and anything can win, while Rainbow View will surely take the Meon Valley Stud Fillies' Mile. Consequently, the Juddmonte Royal Lodge is the only other race to interest me, and **Orizaba** looks a fair price at 4-1.

4.15 Ascot											
Queen Elizabeth II Stakes (Group 1)										1m	

Michael Bell: saddles the improving Furnace

Tom Segal demonstrated his knack of solving big-field sprint handicaps yet again in the Totesport.com Challenge Cup at Ascot in 2009, when his tips finished first and second.

"The Michael Bell-trained Furnace, despite being a year older, is less exposed and came right back to form when winning a competitive race at Chester last time from an outside draw. Furnace was ridden too prominently and didn't get home in the Britannia here last year, but he ran well all the same, which shows he can handle the track, and there is every chance he is still on the upgrade."

Relative Order was the best backed of the Pricewise pair, going off as 9-1 favourite. He led with a furlong to go but was soon overhauled by 12-1 shot Furnace, who held on by a neck under Hayley Turner with the nearest danger to a Pricewise victory – Darryll Holland on We'll Come – three-quarters of a length back in third. Like the Great Yorkshire Chase of 2001, it was a win-win situation for Pricewise followers.

SEA THE STARS (NEWMARKET) – MAY 2, 2009

Tom Segal has discussed in previous chapters how much satisfaction he gains from being the first to identify the potential of a horse or a jockey and he was quick to spot the brilliance of Sea The Stars. Alert *Racing Post* readers will have taken note when, on March 27, he nominated John Oxx's colt as his classic horse to follow in 2009.

"As a half-brother to Galileo, the Derby looks the obvious race for this horse, but he could well be good enough to have a crack at a very open-looking 2,000 Guineas as well," wrote Segal. "Sea The Stars knuckled down well when winning the Group 2 Beresford Stakes on his final start [as a two-year-old] and the attitude he displayed that day will stand him in good stead in all the top races this season."

He had lost none of his enthusiasm for the horse when he came to write his ante-post 2,000 Guineas preview on April 10. As ever, the focus was on Aidan O'Brien's team but Segal wasn't taken by the Ballydoyle market leader. "Unlike the 1,000 Guineas, there is nothing with a totally convincing profile in the colts' version, and the current favourite, Mastercraftsman, is there by default," he wrote. "Stablemate Rip Van Winkle is much classier" and "could well usurp Mastercraftsman as the stable's first string by next month, but he didn't look an easy ride in the Dewhurst.

"My guess is that there is another trainer in Ireland with a much stronger string of three-year-olds this season, and it's not Jim Bolger. John Oxx could be the man to follow, and he intends to saddle two interesting colts in Arazan and Sea The Stars." The latter's performance in the Beresford Stakes had made a big impression on Segal, who argued that "the way he went through the race at The Curragh suggests he could easily be a miler and, at 25-1, he is seriously underestimated by some bookmakers. Of all the top trainers, Oxx is just about the best with a very good horse, and if he thought this was really a mile-and-a-half horse, there is no way he would be contemplating him for the Guineas."

Segal's case concluded: "Sea The Stars could be a really top horse this season, and the 25-1 is too big to miss." By the day of the race, Oxx's superstar-in-waiting had been backed in to 8-1 but he was overshadowed in the market by the 3-1 favourite Delegator, Ballydoyle duo Rip Van Winkle and Mastercraftsman, as well as Sir Michael Stoute's Evasive. As the race unfolded, all eyes were on Delegator, who hit the front with just over a furlong left to run, but Brian Meehan's colt was soon headed by Mick Kinane on Sea The Stars, running on in classy fashion to win by a length and a half.

Segal shared top billing with horse and trainer on the front page of Sunday's *Racing Post*. "Seeing Stars" ran the headline – "Pricewise lands 25-1 knockout blow for bookies as Sea The Stars and trainer John Oxx strike in the 2,000 Guineas."

However, it was a slightly bittersweet moment. "I thought 'oh well, I've done that, I've done Sea The Stars' so the next challenge is to find something to beat him," Segal recalls. "Because after the Guineas and the Derby he'd was always going off at 4-6 or whatever so my job was to find something to beat him which, obviously, I couldn't – nobody could. But every time he ran I'd get a bit of a buzz because I felt I'd spotted something that nobody else had."

As Segal predicted, Sea The Stars turned out to be "a really top horse." He won the Derby at an SP of 11-4, the Eclipse at 4-7, the Juddmonte International at 1-4, the Irish Champion Stakes at 4-6 and, finally, the Arc, also at 4-6. His subsequent dominance makes it hard to fathom how he could ever have been considered a 25-1 shot for any race but that was the price on offer just three weeks before the Guineas – and Pricewise pounced on it.

EVENS AND ODDS (GOODWOOD) – JULY 31, 2010

Goodwood may be one of the most picturesque racecourses in Britain, but it doesn't rank highly on Tom Segal's list of favourite tracks. Asked in a *Racing Post* Twitter Q & A in 2012 to name the racecourses where he has had the least success in his tipping, Segal replied that he was "always rubbish" at Goodwood.

His Pricewise column on July 31, 2010 had an air of resignation about it. "Every year Goodwood is the same," Segal wrote. "Trouble in running for all those horses with fancy trainers and winners galore for the [Richard] Hannon, [Mark] Johnston and Dandy Nicholls yards." Deciding to follow the maxim 'if you can't beat 'em, join 'em', Segal's preview of the Stewards' Cup focused on one of those Goodwood specialists.

The Dandy Nicholls yard was in fine fettle, claiming a 1-2 at Goodwood on Friday as 28-1 shot Joseph Henry led home 13-2 joint-favourite Victoire De Lyphar in the Stewards' Sprint. Nicholls, who had also sent out Hamoody to win the 5f handicap on Thursday, saddled three runners in the Stewards' Cup – Striking Spirit, Sonny Red and Evens And Odds, runner-up in the race 12 months earlier yet available at 33-1 in the morning. Segal assured readers that "there is no way he should be a 33-1 shot given his trainer, his prowess at the course or his form. I think Evens And Odds is at his best on fast ground off a strong pace and, if he can stay in touch early on, I expect him to run a huge race."

Another positive, as far as the price was concerned, was that Evens And Odds was perceived to be badly drawn in stall 18 of 28. Segal's disregard for the impact of the draw was discussed in Chapter Four and his case for Evens And Odds concluded "as for his draw, I haven't noticed any great advantage anywhere this week, and it is worth noting that despite everyone seeming to think a very high draw is imperative, no horse drawn in the 20s has won this race since 2003. Consequently, I have no problems at all with stall 18."

Three other tipsters – Gerald Delamere, Simon Turner of *Racing Post* Ratings and Trading Post's James Pyman – also plumped for Evens And Odds and the tip was a triumph of simplicity – proven course-and-distance performer from an in-form trainer who had already won the race twice before. It was hardly surprising that Evens And Odds caught the attention of punters, who hoovered up the 33-1 and backed it all the way down to 20-1.

Like the *Racing Post* tipsters, jockey Billy Cray kept it simple aboard Evens And Odds. In Sunday's *Post*, reporter Graham Dench described him "storming up the middle of the track to collar far-side leader Jonny Mudball near the finish and win by a neck."

Alongside the race report was a panel of bookmakers' reactions to the Pricewise gamble. David Williams of Ladbrokes called Evens And Odds "an inspired selection" and added "there are many imitations but come Saturday morning there is only one tipster we fear and that is Pricewise." Coral's David Stevens said: "The Stewards' Cup is one of the biggest betting races of the year so to come up with the winner at 33-1 is painful for bookmakers. He's made the difficult look easy."

And Alan Alger, spokesman for race sponsors Blue Square, said: "We were one of the standouts at 33-1. We soon went 28-1 but that didn't last long and nor did 25-1. Although Jonny Mudball was a shorter price, he'd have cost us £60,000 less if he'd held on." It was yet another reminder for bookmakers – as if they needed one – of the power of Pricewise.

RACING POST

Sunday, June 26, 2011 issue No. 8,380 ———— racingpost.com/mobile ———— ON ___ DAY £2.00

50-1 PRICEWISE
THE TOMINATOR

Deadly Tom Segal took aim and fired in another astonishing
big handicap winner, 50-1 Tominator (SP 25-1) in the
Northumberland Plate **Today's 14-1 advice, page 10**

Tipster-turned-action hero Tom Segal gave the bookies a day to forget in June 2011, advising the Northumberland Plater winner Tominator at 50-1.

TOMINATOR (NEWCASTLE) – JUNE 25, 2011

Tom Segal's biggest-priced Pricewise winner came in the 2011 Northumberland Plate when he selected Tominator, the 50-1 outsider of 19, to win the Pitmen's Derby. The ordinary punter might have been comforted if Tom had plumped for Tominator simply because he liked the name but in fact the tip was down to Segal's usual blend of instinct and inspiration.

The headline Pricewise selection for the Plate was Deauville Flyer, a 3-1 favourite for the race in 2010 but available at 10-1 a year later. "Tim Easterby has had this prize earmarked for Deauville Flyer and, with the stable in flying form, the five-year-old should run a big race."

The 7-1 morning co-favourites Overturn, Harlestone Times and Activate were all respected but "at the prices it could be worth taking a flyer on the rank outsider Tominator, who is bred to stay 2m well and every time he runs looks like he's crying out for further. His form when sixth at Newmarket from an unpromising position is solid and he again stayed on well at Haydock last time out [finishing third over 1m 4f on good-to-soft ground]."

Segal's confidence in Tominator was boosted by the parallels with another Pricewise Northumberland Plate hero. "Very soft ground could be a problem for him," he wrote, "but Newcastle was drying quickly last night and he is reminiscent of the brilliant Sergeant Cecil, who took off when upped to this trip in 2005. There is no way he should be a 50-1 shot."

In Chapter Six, several bookmakers spoke about the sinking feeling they get when opening the *Racing Post* on a Saturday morning to discover that they are top price about a Pricewise selection. It isn't hard to imagine, then, the sense of dread hanging over the offices of the two firms – Bet365 and Ladbrokes – who were offering 50-1 about Tominator. And perhaps the phrase 'there but for the grace of God go I' was on the minds of the Stan James compilers who were shortest about Reg Hollinshead's runner at 28-1.

Tominator had predictably halved in price by the start of the Northumberland Plate, going off at an SP of 25-1, although only four of his 18 rivals were a bigger price in the betting. Jockey Paul Pickard, claiming 3lb, settled him in the rear of the field as the previous year's winner Overturn set the pace. However, as Segal had suspected, Tominator relished the step up in trip and moved smoothly through the field to take the lead with a furlong to go, ploughing on to win by a length and three-quarters from 18-1 shot Montaff. The other Pricewise selection, Deauville Flyer, finished third, having "ran a cracker" according to trainer Tim Easterby.

A news piece in the next day's *Racing Post* claimed that the Tominator tip "was estimated to have cost the betting industry more than £1m" and Ladbrokes and Bet365 bore the brunt of Segal's sorcery. Ladbrokes spokesman Alex Donohue said: "Pricewise and his followers have filled us in. The Northumberland Plate is one of the biggest betting handicaps of the summer and it was a desperate result for us, one of the worst in the race for many years."

Pat Cooney of Bet365 managed to see a faint trace of silver lining within the dark, dark cloud. "It was a very poor result," Cooney admitted. "Thankfully, it was a high turnover race with plenty of horses backed, so it could have been worse. A lot of punters also had reverse forecasts with Tom's other selection, Deauville Flyer, so it was at least a relief to see that horse finish third otherwise it would have been a complete disaster."

"Normally, a 25-1 winner of the Northumberland Plate would be good news for the bookies, but having been tipped by Pricewise we've been hit hard by Tominator's victory," said Coral's David Stevens. "Tom Segal has made it look easy once again and the industry faces seven-figure losses as a result of his prowess."

While gloom descended on the bookies, the comments section beneath the race report on the *Racing Post* provided a snapshot of the joy that a big Pricewise gamble brings to punters. "Brilliant Tom Segal. Had £10 e/w at 40-1," enthused one reader while another reported "I backed the two in the Plate at 8-1 and 33-1 – Thanks Tom."

A die-hard Pricewise follower declared: "Segal returns 18 per cent profit over last 5 years if you had backed every selection. I know because I've backed them. Bloke is a genius and has taught me loads by reading his column." "Say what you like but that's some tipping," another contented contributer wrote. "Fair play to Tom Segal! Hope lots of people got on and the bookies took a bashing!" And a Segal supporter employing the time-honoured rhetorical technique of writing in capital letters had the final say: "FACT IS IF YOU BACK EVERY SEGAL HORSE YOU WILL WIN – END OF CHAT."

Sunday's *Racing Post* couldn't resist the obvious Tominator pun. A front-page banner featured Segal mocked up as Arnold Schwarzenegger in the Terminator films, with the caption: 50-1 PRICEWISE THE TOMINATOR. "Deadly Tom Segal took aim and fired in another astonishing big handicap winner, 50-1 Tominator (SP 25-1) in the Northumberland Plate," it explained. Unfortunately for the bookies, Segal, like Arnie, would be back – every Saturday.

EDINBURGH KNIGHT (ASCOT) – OCTOBER 15, 2011

The inaugural Qipco Champions Day took place at Ascot on October 15, 2011 and Segal wasn't immune to the hype. "Any day the undisputed world miling champion Frankel struts his stuff is a great day in my book," he wrote, "and the supporting cast would top most other bills too, with the Group 1 winners So You Think, Midday, Twice Over, Snow Fairy and Nathaniel all locking horns in the Champion Stakes."

The quality of the fields assembled at Ascot was not in doubt but it was a tricky card for Segal. Punters and bookmakers were well acquainted with the major players and it looked like a day to marvel at Europe's greatest flat horses rather than plot a handicap coup.

"Frankel is the only place to start and all things being equal he should win the QEII," Segal wrote. However, Sir Henry Cecil's star was no bigger than 1-2 with Ladbrokes – and just 2-7 with Coral – in the morning. The

Pricewise column concluded that there wasn't much leeway for punters in the Champion Stakes, either: "So You Think is my idea of the winner as I would imagine Aidan O'Brien has tailored his season for an autumn campaign, but do I think the 3-1 is anything to write home about? Probably not."

The first Pricewise tip of the day came up against another Ballydoyle superstar, Fame And Glory, as well as morning favourite Opinion Poll and impressive Newmarket winner Times Up, in the British Champions Long Distance Cup. Nehaam had been beaten by Times Up last time out but liked Ascot and, Segal wrote, "I wouldn't be surprised if John Gosden's charge reversed the placings." Given that Times Up was 7-2 in the early prices and Nehaam was a 33-1 chance, the Gosden horse looked cracking value and punters agreed, backing it in to 12-1 by the start of the race.

Nehaam did indeed reverse placings with Times Up, finishing fourth, two lengths ahead of the 100-30 shot. It was a moral victory for Pricewise – the 33-1 shot was just touched off for second and was only a length and a quarter behind the winner, Fame And Glory – but more tangible rewards would come later in the day.

The *Racing Post* analysis of the Future Stars Apprentice Handicap sniffed that "it was a bit of a shame that such a cracking card featuring so many top-class horses should conclude with a humdrum handicap for apprentices." Pricewise followers had no reason to complain, however, as Edinburgh Knight, advised at 33-1 and sent off at 18-1, held on under jockey Matthew Davies and Castles In The Air, who was backed from 40-1 in to 12-1, took third, finishing first on the far side.

Segal conceded that the Apprentice Handicap "looks a bit odd rounding off such a tremendous card, but it is my type of race and there are a couple at massive prices who are worth backing." The 29-runner handicap was a classic Pricewise race and Castles In The Air and Edinburgh Knight were classic Segal tips, relying on his "feel" for both the horses and the market. His reasoning for both was straightforward. Castles In The Air "is very good at this track and ran a cracker here a few starts back [...] he's now 8lb lower than when winning a similar race over course and distance last season." Paul D'Arcy's Edinburgh Knight "hasn't enjoyed the rub of the green in the top sprint handicaps" but "if he returns to his best he has more than enough ability to win."

Edinburgh Knight did get back to his best and Castles In The Air finished third, just a nose away from landing a remarkable 1-2 for Pricewise. Frankel's demolition of his rivals in the Queen Elizabeth II Stakes may have been the outstanding performance on Champions Day but Segal's effort in the final race on the card wasn't far behind.

HURRICANE HIGGINS & SIR GRAHAM WADE (GOODWOOD) – AUGUST 1, 2012

Segal makes no secret of his dislike of Goodwood from a punting perspective. In 2012, therefore, he decided to put his trust in trainer Mark Johnston, a man who has seemingly solved the riddle of the Sussex Downs. This policy paid off in fine style on the Wednesday of Glorious Goodwood as Pricewise – ably assisted by Johnston – pulled off a 434-1 double in the day's big-field handicaps.

Even so, Segal's column that day started with the admission that "Mark Johnston is a trainer I have never been able to get right. His horses simply don't run to a normal profile, but there are two reasons why we must be wary of his runners today: the form he is in and the track they are running at."

"Take your cue and pocket the cash with Hurricane Higgins" advised the Pricewise headline but Johnston's stayer, like his snooker-playing namesake, was far from straightforward. He was only running at Goodwood because he had failed a stalls test at Catterick the week before and the 2m 5f Goodwood Stakes was started by tape.

Segal looked beyond this quirk, however, and focused on Hurricane Higgins's ability, concluding that he was "massively overpriced" at 28-1 with Hills. "He is a class above his opposition if he does get the trip and his pedigree suggests he might well be a stayer. There is no better trainer of a staying horse than Johnston, who sent out Hurricane Higgins's half-brother Jukebox Jury to dead-heat in the Irish St Leger and win a Group race in France over two miles, so I'm pretty sure Hurricane Higgins will appreciate a step up in trip. If he does stay he could be in a different class to his rivals."

Backed into 14-1, Hurricane Higgins did indeed appreciate the longest race of the week, travelling well throughout under Joe Fanning and holding off a late charge from Defence Of Duress (ridden by Segal's favourite handicap jockey Jamie Spencer) to win by a neck.

It was Mark Johnston's 52nd winner at Glorious Goodwood and the Middleham trainer didn't have long to wait until No. 53. Johnston's Scatter Dice was the 8-1 joint-favourite for the UBS Stakes in the morning, alongside Rule Book, but Segal was more taken by the chances of bottom-weight Sir Graham Wade at a general 14-1.

"He has been off the track since April but has always been considered a horse with a ton of potential," Segal wrote. "There is a chance he is still not streetwise enough for a race like this, but I can't believe a rating of 80 is anything like the limit of what he is capable of and, given the form of the yard and his price, he is well worth backing.

Following what Segal described as "Frankel's exercise gallop" – Sir Henry Cecil's star won the Sussex Stakes by six lengths at an SP of 1-20 – Sir Graham Wade, whose morning price of 14-1 didn't shorten, saw off his 15 rivals in convincing fashion. His trainer told reporters afterwards that he was "a classic stayer in the making" – a quote that backed up Segal's pre-race claims about his potential.

After Goodwood, the racing world moves on to York, Doncaster and Newmarket, and from there to the Prix de l'Arc de Triomphe and the embryonic tradition of Ascot's Champions Day. The jumps season picks up momentum at Newbury, Sandown, Kempton and Chepstow, culminating in the Cheltenham Festival, the Grand National and Punchestown. The flat returns with the Lincoln and Newmarket's Guineas meeting before attention turns to Chester, Epsom and Royal Ascot.

Mel Collier calls it "the natural rhythm to the season" and he believes that Pricewise has become "a part of that rhythm." For as long as punters are more interested in what wins tomorrow than what won ten years ago, tipsters – with Pricewise, hopefully, leading the way – will continue to play their part in the rhythm of the seasons.

INDEX